Why is the Handicapped Stall the Very Last One in the Row?

(UNABRIDGED VERSION)

Why is the Handicapped Stall the Very Last One in the Row?

Please Come and ~~Walk~~ With Me

This journal provides an inside look at the many difficulties
the disabled endure
every minute, every hour, every moment,
and every movement

Tory Sileo

To order additional copies of this book, contact:
Xlibris Corporation
1-888-795-4274
www.Xlibris.com
Orders@Xlibris.com
75358

Contents

Preface

There were many reasons that prompted me to sit down to begin writing this journal. My first reason was to try to quiet the constant internal conversations that have tormented me. I cannot accept this disease. Every movement is difficult. Simple personal grooming, mundane to most, such as taking a shower, or a feat as trivial as brushing my teeth is a struggle, and every step becomes a monumental episode. My constant bowel and bladder problems prevent me from attending any "spur of the moment" events. I am hesitant to plan back-to-back activities. Two events in one day are usually too exhausting for me, causing me to limit my scheduling. Each day has to be planned and thought out. This speculation is a major disruption on my life. There is always concern about what will happen, when will it happen, or how bad can it get. These are the fears that encompass my every thought. I hoped that maybe, if I were able to share them, my mind would be able to put my fears into language and allow my heart and soul to rest.

I also felt that the time had finally come where I could shed some honesty on my real daily struggles. One doctor told me to begin writing down my daily aches and pains resulting from my injections and their side effects. Since my diagnosis with Multiple Sclerosis, I have allowed only a few people into my inner circle to share the struggles that I endure every day. I did not want to go through my life with people feeling sorry for me. I do not want to feel pitied. I tried to hide my MS as long as I possibly could. As of today, however, the disease has become obvious to any who watches me walk or slur my words, particularly when I am tired. They understand my inability to readily recall information that my brain received as recently as one hour prior. On days where focusing is an issue, my brain may not recall asking the same question that was asked and answered five minutes prior.

Friends and family have labeled me both stubborn and proud. I must admit that I have refused help when I really needed it. I refused assistance—help that was graciously offered—and help that I should have accepted. I felt so very ashamed to. More often than not, I took one step, and fell to the ground quickly and without warning. I labeled this my Rag Doll Syndrome. My muscles were lifeless and useless. I did not have enough strength to stand up again. My falling frustrated those that offered help. I was embarrassed as I attempted to lift myself up from the floor. My intention was not to push anyone away; my foolishness is a direct result of the independent side of me. My pride has gotten in the way of my common sense. I have found it extremely difficult to accept this horrendous disease. It strikes any part of my body at any time. I must admit, now, in all honesty, my fear of my losing control of my own body is always overwhelming and will forever be frightening.

Finally, I will share some difficulties that I have encountered as a disabled person. Most of them will enlighten you, as they have me. Some of them may anger you, but most of them will stop you in your tracks as you go through even one day of the obstacles that the handicapped endure despite the rules and regulations of the American Disability Act. Accommodations and provisions for those of us that are less capable should come from one's heart, not from a set of bylaws being forced upon the able bodied.

In summary, this book discusses nothing with the hopes of accomplishing everything. You might listen in to our internal frustrations or may for a moment feel our pain.

This story marks the sad ending of my life as I once knew and enjoyed it. Today here and now, my new life begins. I stride to accept my increasingly necessary modifications to once again enjoy life.

Tory Sileo

I wish to extend my sincerest thanks to those of you who have been there to assist me despite my foolish, stubborn, and independent ways.

My gratitude extends to my caring and kind neurologist, who has seen me at my worst and has always helped me to feel my best.

My special thanks extend to the staff of Central Five School for their kindness and support when I needed it the most. K, little sister, thanks for your extra special efforts. I know you were living the torment with me.

A warm hug goes out to dear friend B, who cared enough to ask and understand my behind-the-scene difficulties of living with this devil-like spirit called MS.

Then there is Arbeeo, who can always be found on the sidelines handing me a miracle drink from the nearest health food store.

Of course, my love and gratitude goes to my husband, my caretaker, and my soul mate. He has had to dramatically alter his life and truly understands that we both have MS. He continues to be my strength, will forever be the air that I breathe, and will always hold the key to my heart.

Why is the Handicapped Stall the Very Last One?

If you have had an opportunity to cross my path and we have chatted, you already know that I am a stubborn woman with a disability that, up to this very moment, I have refused to truly accept. My feelings are not unique, and it can be said that most persons with any degree of disability, initially attempt to live their life as if their diagnosis did not disable them. There comes a moment in time, perhaps an incident, where the disability becomes larger than life. It was one of those moments, for me, when I had to concede and acknowledge my illness.

Admitting defeat meant that I needed to graciously accept assistance and to stop those famous last words, "No, I can do it." As I am being lifted from the floor, it has become obvious to all that no, I could not have done it. That terrifying moment, when the realization of the consequences of my disease finally struck home, was devastating for me. I live with overwhelming fear.

As my disease is progressing, I have been extremely surprised by some of the obstacles that I have run into as I attempt to travel through life with some limitations. Please allow me to share one blatant, rather funny experience with you, and jokingly I am sure that you too will agree:

Why is the handicapped stall in the ladies' room the farthest from the entry door?

Recently, I watched a woman who had suffered a stroke and had no feeling in her right extremities. Her daughter helped her into the ladies' room. The handicapped stall was the last one in a row of ten. Her mom's apparent exhaustion did not come from the facilities' noncompliance with ADA regulations; it simply came from the designer's lack of understanding and compassion for the disabled person's challenges.

I have found that in most places where there is a public restroom, the handicapped stall is the last one in the row. The disabled person's stall, equipped with bars to balance, should be the first stall as you enter the room. The dictionary definition of disability is "restricted capability to perform particular activities, medical condition restricting activities, payment to person with inability, legal disqualifier." Attempting to thrust myself forward another ten yards can be paralleled to climbing the tallest mountain by an able body individual.

So, once again I ask, why would the use of the handicapped stall require additional walking?

I know you will chuckle and think about the question the next time you use a public restroom I have found that nine out of ten handicapped stalls are indeed located at the end of the row of stalls.

Tuesday, February 12

My husband is home today. He is off of work for a holiday, but to tell you the truth, at this very moment, I cannot recall which holiday it is. Short-term memory has become a problem for me. I do not share this with my husband. It is just another symptom of this horrible disease called Multiple Sclerosis. As the minutes or hours pass, I usually will remember. Until then, only the nagging voice inside my head will know. My lack of recall, something as simple as why he has off, is both astounding and frightening.

My husband has suddenly become a caretaker, and alone must handle the everyday household and financial obligations. Watching me fade away, both mentally and physically, has taken a lot out of him. He looks drained and tired.

Wednesday, February 13

It is a difficult time for me right now. It is becoming obvious that I may not be able to continue working. My body is turning on me in such a way that I just may not be able to do much of anything, especially teach.

I am a teacher now and knew I wanted to be a teacher since I was in the eighth grade. The upper-grade students were honored to select a younger-grade class and to spend the day with them. We were allowed to be their teacher for that day. I do not remember what it was that I taught them, but I do know that my career in the field of education was born on that special day.

I was raised in an era where students graduated college in four years, went on for a Master's Degree in two to three years, were gainfully employed while achieving their Master's and out of the nest and living on their own. It perplexes me when I hear of a student dropping out of college to "find themselves," or who takes five or six years to earn enough credits to graduate. I find myself wondering if they met with a guidance counselor before entering college. How about during their college years? How many of us old timers were asked, "So what do you want to be when you grow up?" What happened to that timeless expression?

There is a huge difference between a "job" and a "career." Our young people need to embrace that distinction earlier in their lives. Someone needs to guide them along the way. The "what do you want to be . . ." conversation may be a good starting point. Suddenly, I have found that the college graduates in my family and my friend's children have finally graduated but without direction or intent. I am sure that you can relate to my story in one way or another, but let's continue our earlier thoughts.

I woke up at my usual 5:30 AM, did the whole prepare-for-work routine, ate breakfast, and left my home to drive to work by 6:30 AM. This one hour every day was exhausting for me. It took approximately twenty-five minutes to drive to my school.

The drive was much easier for me when it was light outside, early fall and the spring daylight hours. I was finding it very difficult to drive in what I call "dark morning" or "dark afternoon." The streetlights or vehicle headlights had a "halo" around them. One light appeared as two lights or one large blurred illumination. I could not tell anyone about my difficulty. I was certain that my driving days were limited. I was not, however, ready to lose the feeling of independence, a privilege that driving allowed me. Truth be told, I must share that the twenty-five-minute car ride to work was really becoming a chore. I was finding it difficult to see as clearly as I should.

One morning, a monthly calendar appeared on my desk. Each day of the month had another teacher's name was handwritten into the box. My colleagues had joined together and formed a car pool. The name in the box was my "Driver of the Day." Suddenly, I had a ride home from school each school day by a different colleague. I felt extremely honored to be a part of this faculty. They were taking their time, using their gas and energy to volunteer for this commitment. Their compassion was overwhelming and I was beyond humbled. On one hand, I was thankful for their help, driving was becoming increasingly difficult. Yet it feels surreal to me when I even consider the notion of not being able to drive.

My school consisted of two separate buildings connected with a breezeway. There were days and weeks that could pass without me even seeing one of my colleagues. The ride home from school with a different colleague gave both of us a chance to chitter-chatter. My aunt coined that phrase. That is always, even today, how she described her day with her senior friends. I consider myself fortunate to have worked with such caring people. After working a full day, most of us just want to go home. My "limo drivers" put their needs after mine. Their after-school activities were put on hold for an hour or so. We both enjoyed the time together, but a part of me always felt guilty for taking "the Driver of the Day" away from their own lives.

Wednesday, February 13

It is approximately 7:00 AM. I have safely arrived, but the first item on the list is to sit, well actually, collapse, into my chair. I made it to work and am proud of myself. I try to ignore that little voice shouting out to me.

"You can't walk! You really can't drive! You can't see! You can't remember! You have MS! You are not well! Your idea of managing this illness is naive. You have MS!"

As usual, I dismiss and ignore the little voice. I am proud of myself for even getting this far, and with frustration and fortitude resulting from my anger, I stand up from my chair, take my coat off, lock up my pocketbook, put my lunch in the refrigerator in the teachers' room, and return to my desk. How much longer can I do this? I am already exhausted and my day has not really begun.

I review my plan book, write tonight's homework on the blackboard, and retrieve the necessary tools needed to prepare for the day's objective. I finally move on to noting how I will "hook" the students. What will be my introduction of the new skill so that the process is animated and more easily remembered and grasped by my students? Maybe today will be one of those days where my assessment of their newly acquired skill can be taught to the rest of the class by one of the students.

This procedure is a good idea, and as I continue, it becomes obvious that my students become impassioned. When a student can teach a skill that they have learned, I can easily assess their concept of the new skill. I am a very animated teacher, not one that teaches from her desk chair. I am currently afraid to walk around for fear of falling in front of my students, but anything less than being 'in their face' is not my style of teaching. I have found that for me anyway, animation keeps their attention. I love to watch each student grasp the objective at different times, and in different ways. They, the students, my kids are the reason I feel compelled to stay.

Today once again, I must admit slipping away to myself my difficulties and acknowledge that I am. Teaching is not a job, but rather my career, and I am determined to fight to stay with a fierce, ambitious drive.

I just realized that I forgot to call the main office to inform them that I am here on the premises and ask someone to please bring down my mail. Asking someone to go out of their way, again, for me is just another example of the accommodations done on my behalf. My hopes are that I can continue to teach. Teaching is a fastidious career, despite those who continually recite the 'summers off' song. It has been difficult to accept help and even more difficult to accept the fact that I can no longer accomplish what I was able to do before it myself.

When I had been capable of accomplishing and completing whatever I wanted to do and I was without MS, it always made me feel satisfied whenever I was able, to help or assist someone. If I follow that same line of reasoning to those that help me, I therefore should not feel guilty and accept their help graciously. Accepting assistance, auspiciously and without guilt, is difficult for me.

Back to my morning and the start of my teaching day: I usually bring a thermos of coffee to work because I cannot drink it in the morning before work. I did not drink anything before driving to work simply because I would need to use the bathroom before making it into the building. It is only a twenty-five-minute drive but for my bladder, it feels like an eternity. An overactive bladder gave me the feeling of having to urinate even when I used the bathroom only seven minutes prior. This constant interruption was ludicrous and could not continue!

Here is a side story and seems to be ridiculous even to me: Before I was diagnosed, I had that feeling of urgency but did not know why. I had no medication to suppress the feeling because I had not been to see a urologist. My parents, my husband, and I went to Animal Kingdom Park. There we were driving through, following the map given to us at the entrance gate.

Shortly after we began the drive-through, I had that sense of urgency and needed to use the ladies' room. Stop and think for a moment; we are inside the gates where the animals live. We have invaded their space. Visitors to the park were instructed to remain in their cars with the windows closed. The longer it took to get some Park Ranger assistance, the harder it was "to hold it in" and the more frightened I became. I was very concerned of having an "accident." How embarrassing would it be if I were unable to control my bladder in public!

We asked another ranger, who pointed to a porta-potty and told us that was the closest one but it was only for Park Rangers and that park patrons weren't allowed out of their cars. Her instructions continued on to those that were still in the car; I was long gone to the port-a-potty while she continued her speech. It all comes down to one very familiar phrase: "When ya gotta go, ya gotta go."

I had to go. I have not had the opportunity to visit the Animal Kingdom again. I would not have that problem again; now I do see a urologist and am on medication. It amazes me even today as to how many body parts and their functions we all take for granted.

Walking is another function that we take for granted. Before my diagnosis, and even afterward, I would walk around the building whenever I had free time without my students. Another teacher walked with me. We wore pedometers and were very diligent in our exercise regime. We clocked our strides, distance, and calories used. Most of the staff knew that Mike and I were walking buddies. Mike and I stopped our walking together; he continued to walk, and I could walk only short distances. Presently, there are some days that I cannot walk at all; there are other days when I cannot even stand without falling.

When I stopped walking around the building with Mike, I could see and feel the sense of sadness in the eyes of my colleagues. I knew what they were thinking. Just a short time ago, she was walking around the school building, these days she can't even walk to the office.

I knew what they were remembering. I was remembering too. I know that they are genuinely saddened when they witness my diminished abilities now. My apparent lack of ability to balance myself speaks volumes when no words are spoken.

They have offered to walk my class to the cafeteria for lunch and to lead them into the building in the morning. They have assisted me whenever possible. They offered to bring my class to their daily specials, including activities such as music, gym, art, computer, and the like. Yes indeed, my limited walking has, was, and still is obvious to all.

For many years before I finally had a conclusive diagnosis of MS, various doctors attempted to treat my ailments. None of them listened to my symptoms and were able to come to a conclusive diagnosis. In the past, I have been diagnosed with the Epstein-Barr virus, Chronic Fatigue Syndrome, Lupus, and MS. Now, some twenty-plus years later, my diagnosis of MS was the correct one. I have been taking injections for eight years now. Multiple Sclerosis has dealt me a hand that is charged with the most difficult of challenges. There are moments when I can vividly recall the fear that came over me as a little girl when I had to see my pediatrician. I cried and cried and was frozen with fear when just the thought of an injection was a possibility. The reward I received, we all received, that stupid lollipop afterward, did not lessen the fear or the pain. Today, I inject myself, a shocking notion, especially to me. And still today, even larger Tootsie-Roll Lollipops, do not lessen my anxieties concerning needles.

Friday, February 15

My students are about to enter my classroom. My ambulating is very limited. Another teacher is walking them into the school building; the start of the school day is about to begin. My students know what procedure they have to follow. It is well into the school year. Everyone knows what is expected of them during their time in the morning homeroom. Most them follow homeroom prodigal, most of them. I remind those students of the procedure they should be following. I would like to proudly announce that after the second reminder, all of them comply, but I cannot. As I look around the classroom, nine out of ten are on task. I am pleased with the 90 percent. As their teacher, I follow the motto known as "pick and choose your battles"; 90 percent is excellent. I will talk privately with the other 10 percent.

The first academic period of the day is about to begin; it is 8:30 AM. Language Arts is the academic area that I teach to two different two classes, my class and my partner's class.

Every teacher has a different method of delivery. Primarily, as I have already shared I use humor to keep my students focused and attentive. I move around the classroom while I teach. An effective teacher has to grab the students' attention from the first word she utters. I am walking around, moving from desk to desk, and my delivery of the day's Language Arts objective is crystal clear. Each student is attentive, wondering where and what I will do next.

It is almost 10:00 AM. I will have a forty-five-minute rest and I need every second of it. Someone will bring my class back into the classroom, and Social Studies will begin.

The remainder of this school day continues as usual. Different subjects, different objectives, different deliveries, but the same energy is necessary through out the day. I am frustrated. I suddenly feel unsteady and am experiencing a balancing problem. This is when I become concerned that I may fall with my students present in the classroom. This is just another conversation going on in my mind. Tonight I need a good night's sleep. The truth of the matter is this: more sleep may or may not make a difference tomorrow.

Wednesday, February 20

I arrived at school a little earlier today. I need some quiet time to prepare some paperwork before my students arrive. It is a "dark morning," and the drive to school was not an easy one. There are very few teachers' cars in the lot. It scares me. There was a time when I arrived early because the weather guru had predicted an icy morning commute. It began to flurry with freezing temperatures during my drive to school. I was nervous and quite proud of myself for having made it to school without incident. I opened my driver's door, stepped one step out of the car, and slipped on the ice. No one was around, and my MS rendered me weak. I sat on the ground until the first teacher arrived. She stopped her car the moment she saw me sitting on the ground and ran over to help me up. I never shared that with anyone and had no intention of sharing it. She did inform my Principal and the news spread from there.

It is almost the end of the marking period and I need to enter additional test grades into my computer. My students understand the concept of averaging. I have a conference with them individually to discuss their grades and allow them to calculate their average. Their input and their own calculations give them the opportunity to receive a higher grade. This method works well for the students who are on the cusp between two grades.

Today was a school day that began as all days had begun for over a decade of teaching and ended as none had before. I drove to school today with my students' grades along with my computer. Completing my student's grade averaging and conferencing with them individually were the main issues on my daily agenda. As it turned out, it would be my last day as a teacher employed with my current school district. I had a meeting scheduled with my Superintendent. Our meeting focused primarily on my declining health issues. We discussed my MS and its apparent decline into the Secondary Progressive Phase. He shared with me his concern about my falling in the parking lot and in the classroom. He encouraged me to enjoy quality time at home with my family and not in a classroom. In the privacy of my imagination, I agreed with him. He knew how important my pride was to me. My mind ran through my daily incapacities and his suggestion was more than palpable. It took everything I had to muster up my agreement.

It is true that perhaps I could slow down the progression if I did not have the stress of working. There was a certain irony in play in my silence. Together, he and I came to the same conclusion. Today would be my last day, and we could use whatever sick days I have accumulated to get my full pay between now and the end of the school year. He told me that I did not even have to finish out the day. As of this very minute, I have been extricated. I left his office and limped to my car. I sat in it, trying to unravel the last hour. Is it over? Just like that? What about my kids? How would I tell them? What would I tell them?

I looked at my watch and calculated the timing. When I returned to my school building, my students would be at lunch. I swaggered back to my classroom, solicited the help of another teacher, and as quickly as we could, we removed and packed personal items from my desk. Our goal was to pack as much as possible and be out before my students came back from their lunch and recess. In a rushed forty-five minutes, I was packed and gone.

I pulled over at the first opportunity, sat in my car, and told myself that I was no longer employed as a teacher, starting here and right now. I would not have to wake up at 5:30 tomorrow morning. I would not have to make my lunch tonight or rummage through my clothing, looking for an outfit to wear to work. As of today, it was over. I slowly drove home, almost trancelike. I have been officially extricated.

As a result of my being home without anyone around, my husband immediately ordered a MedicAlert device for me to wear. "Help me, I've fallen and I can't get up." I can't believe I have become that woman in that old commercial. If you do not remember that commercial, you are younger than me.

I thought back over my thirty-year career in the field of education. I remembered where it started, as a public school teacher. Today, it ended as a public school teacher. The years in between were more than I could have ever hoped for. After I graduated with a Bachelor of Arts degree, I continued with my education, earning a Master's Degree in the field of Administration and Supervision in Education. I continued on and went into the Private Education sector as the Director for close to two decades. The school grew and went on to receive many awards and acknowledgements. I continued on with my education and earned credits toward my doctorate.

Today, it was over. In one hour's meeting, the inevitable has happened. I knew in my heart the day that I fell in the classroom with my students' present was the final step. The sudden fall came as it usually had, fast, quick, instantaneous and without warning. Another teacher was in my classroom as additional support for forty five minutes one time a week. It was unfathomable that the fall occurred within that same time frame. She helped me up as quickly as possible. I saw the fear in my students' eyes. I did what I usually would do, turn it into a humorous moment and asked the closest student why he pushed me. Soon, the students were laughing and their fears were arrested for the moment, Two falls, the parking lot and the classroom turned me into a liability risk for the district and my children. My internal desultory conversation could not be silenced.

Tomorrow would come and I had no class, no school, and no one to teach. I am aware that the time has come for me to slow down, recognize what I can still do, and say out loud, "I am disabled." A profound sense of sadness came over me.

People have since asked me how I am. How does it feel not to teach? Do you miss it? However I respond, they quickly add, "Just wait until the dust settles and next September rolls around, do you think you will miss it then?" I do not miss the paperwork, and I do enjoy being able to use a bathroom whenever the moment strikes. I do not miss the 5:30-6:30 AM "dark morning marathons," but I do enjoy being able to make a telephone call whenever I need to. What I began to miss a few weeks back, what I miss now, and what I will always miss is my interaction with my students, our mutual respect for each other, and the joy that only children can provide. I will always miss the look on their faces when they finally understood what they may have struggled to understand in the past. What I have accomplished in my career and the difference that I may have made in the life of a student is what all educators miss once they leave the field of education. I am not unique; most career educators miss their students, and most continue to have communications with students long after the teacher has retired and the student becomes an adult.

Monday, February 25

Dealing with Multiple Sclerosis and its many symptoms is nothing short of "reaching into the sky, attempting to catch a falling star." When I woke up this morning, I felt perfectly fine. It was only 5:15. I got up and showered. I joined my husband at the breakfast table. I had an appointment with my Superintendent. I asked him to sign a few documents that needed to be included in my application packet being forwarded onto my Pension Disability Division. The meeting was short, and the drive to and from the Superintendent's office was without complications.

By the time I returned home, I barely made it up the steps to my bedroom. I could not walk. I could not stand without falling. When I did fall, I did not have the strength or energy to stand up again. I tried to use a makeshift pulley out of the sheets or comforter or whatever to pull myself up. Every "tool" I made to help pull myself up with failed, and I kept falling backward with total frustration. This feeling rendered the muscles in my lower back useless. I was totally incompacitated. My pain was immeasurable.

I had no choice but to push the button on my MedicAlert bracelet. The voice box was the top of the staircase landing, and the only way for me to shout into it was to crawl to where it would hear me. The emergency alert personnel asked me what I needed, and I told them that I simply could not get off of the floor. Unbelievable to me, I truly used the button and shouted those famous words, "Help me, I've fallen and I can't get up." It was so similar to that famous commercial. If I wasn't so frightened and frustrated, I, too, would have laughed but my deflated ego prevented finding the humor. The first person on my emergency contact list was my neighbor and close friend. Luckily, she was home, came over, and assisted me in getting up off of the floor and back into my bed. She sat at the foot of my bed for a few minutes, and we chatted about nothing. When she left, I cried like a baby! The day started and ended so very differently. What was ultimately going to happen to me?

Tuesday, February 26

I do not want to spend any time on the floor unable to get up by myself. I woke up tired and am already having difficulty walking. I was scheduled to meet with my Principal today for more paperwork, signatures, and more letters. Today for the first time, I realized that I just could not do what I had planned to do. Dressing, driving, walking, and even talking seemed out of my range of ability. I made a phone call to reschedule and went back to bed.

Thursday, February 28

Today, I am rescheduled to see both my Principal and Superintendent for their completion of additional documents required for my disability income packets. So far, this morning I am feeling strong enough to drive to their offices and back home again. I cannot do anything else prior to driving there for fear of losing the stamina I have right now.

I have returned home, but as I type this, my right hand is tingling and is becoming less and less operational. I can't type anymore. This will be my last sentence for today.

Tuesday, March 11

My husband took off of work today so he can drive me to see my neurologist. It is a joint appointment because we both want to hear and understand what is happening to me. I have completely stopped taking my new injection every other day. My body has rejected it twice already. The drug rendered me unable to do nothing more than lie in bed sleeping.

When I was awake, I fell more times than not. I had started it at a higher dosage and became deathly sick. I tried a lesser dose after a two-week hiatus after the first treatment almost killed me. Even with the lesser dose, my body did not accept the drug and my reaction was a near-death experience.

I have researched the medical options that are available for Secondary Progressive MS. There are none. The current medications are best suited for Relapsing-Remitting MS. Doctors diagnosing Secondary Progressive MS feel that a stronger medication is better, sometimes two medications at the same time is best. I have had major side effects from some medications that I have taken in the past. The new drug for MS has been on and off the market. That drug is one option for me; it involves a monthly transfusion of Tysabri. It scares me. At this time, for me anyway, Tysabri has yet to prove its validity as a drug to slow down the progression of MS.

Wednesday, March 12

My neurologist did not have good news for me. It went as I had anticipated. More drugs, perhaps a combination thereof might help slow down the progression but their side effects were just short of lethal. Wasn't that visit fun?

Today I also received a phone call from my Principal. He wanted to be the first one to inform me that I was selected to receive the honor of "Teacher of the Year." I might have been honored to achieve this award last year or next year. Deep down in my soul, I felt that I was being honored because people felt sorry for me. Are they trying to lift my spirits? Either way, I have had the privilege of working side by side with very considerate people. Perhaps this is just another example of their kindness.

Thursday, March 13

We just received a frightening call. A very close friend of over thirty years was calling from an ambulance. He was in the middle of a meltdown, a near nervous breakdown. He called the ambulance himself because he had suicidal thoughts. He lost his wife a short time ago; she died next to him in bed in the middle of the night. She had a massive heart attack and was gone. His is a very dear friend, and his suicidal thoughts have saddened my husband and me. Tomorrow, we will see him at the hospital. We will continue to support him. Thirty years is a long time.

Sunday, March 23

I am very lucky to have such a wonderful support system. Today was a quiet and restful day. That same settled and tranquil feeling came over me. Family and friends stopped by to say hello and give me an endearing hug. Of course, the usual questions about my missing teaching came up along with the assurances of my own future meltdown once September rolls around. My answer is always the same, but no one really hears or believes me. It is the fiercely difficult grind of the day that was the most problematic for me.

The relationships that I built with my students are what I already miss. I have missed them since I made my hasty and unexpected exit. September does not fit into the equation right now. I am dealing with new medication and a worsened diagnosis. I am always concerned about tomorrow. I close my eyes with a fear of waking up tomorrow morning blind or not being able to feel my feet, or any number of horrid possibilities. I do not share my fear with my friends or family, I see no reason to worry them. We will all deal with the symptoms as they come along.

Tonight I received a telephone call on my cell phone from a parent of one of my favorite students. John is a boy who is extremely sensitive and bright. Earlier in the school year, I have had to shield him as they attempted to some of the other boys from bully him. Of course, I put a stop to such behavior, but it was an issue that I was constantly aware of. Without a word being uttered to any student, John was able to go and come without fear, and his enjoyment of our one year school continued to thrive.

The telephone call was from his mom. He was apparently having a difficult time. John missed me so very much and was now having a bad experience in his class. The students weren't learning, the class itself had no direction, and the objectives necessary for the students to be exposed to for the state test were not being covered. She felt that all of the necessary testing skills needed to achieve a higher score were not being met. Her question to me was simple: "Would I be returning soon?" She questioned his new teacher's curriculum, and felt that her son's need for exposure to many of the skills required for his achievement was simply not being met.

Perhaps her concerns were real ones. The permanent substitute that replaced me was young and right out of college. I was certain that my wise-guy boys were running the classroom. A first-year permanent substitute, I was sure, was having a difficult time with regard to behavior, not to mention my accelerated curriculum program.

My reply was a difficult one. I wanted to return, if even for a day, to speak to the class—the boys in particular. I needed to return to let the class know what was happening. They deserved an answer. Remember, I was taken from them in the middle of the day without warning. They returned from their lunch and I was not there. They knew my car; that day, and each day after and realized I was not there. Since I had driven to work less and less, my car's not being there was still not a definite conclusion as to whether I was in the classroom as they arrived. Their misbehaviors were predictable and most probable. Their world was turned upside down.

John finally did get on the telephone. He told me that he missed me and couldn't bear the thought of completing the school year without my being there. It saddened me to tell him that I would not return. I could feel his tremors and disappointment through the phone. I finally was able to tell both him and his mom that I would not be returning.

Once he hung up the extension, I was able to explain to his mom the whys of my not being able to return. I shared my diagnosis. I could feel her tears, as I am sure she could feel mine. I had made a difference in her son's life, and suddenly his academic life was speculative. How could he grasp any of this, he was only ten years old?

John's number has made it to my cell phone, and we will continue our relationship once this school year was over. I had to stay away and let the new teacher find her own method of dealing with my class, wise guys, sensitive students, and others who made up the mix of twenty-six students, collectively know as Homeroom #29.

This call clarified my feeling. I must return to my class and give them a proper good-bye and an overdue explanation. They are only ten old children. As I have explained to those who remind me of my feelings when September rolls around, I will not miss the arduous, regimented, difficult physical routine. I miss my interaction with my students and my being able to be there for their nonacademic needs. I will speak to the teacher and select a day where I can go to the class with her permission and without any advance notice to the students. There are quite a few loose ends to tie up.

Today is a day that must be one of total accomplishments. My new desk (once having been a dining room table), along with all of the paperwork involved in handling seven different files, must be cleaned up. How can I have an Open House with clutter? Files, empty boxes, a garage filled with packed boxes, and items that are not going with us but rather to the Goodwill store for donation must be somehow organized. The phrase 'organized chaos' once again, comes to mind.

I just received my dreaded phone call from a nurse representing another drug company that my doctor has insisted on my trying. She seemed pleasant enough, but briefly explained that this injection is not premixed and she will go through the steps necessary prior to injecting myself. It sounds anything but pleasant. Secondary Progressive MS does not have other options at this time. I am just a mere beach ball bouncing around in the ocean, being taken by the winds and the waves and without the slightest control over my destiny.

My husband, who has always been a planner, has scheduled every major event in his life, his marriage, his children, and his many years of employment. It is extremely difficult for him to accept and become the ball being tossed around. His lack of control has affected the very core of his being. Both of my stepchildren are aware of his difficulties and, together, as a family, have made his challenges just a little easier. I have also discussed his dilemma with his best friend. He would have been the first one I called, but he has his own problems with the possibility of his wife's cancer spreading.

Tuesday, March 25

I had my first physical therapy session today. My neurologist prescribed this mode of treatment in an effort to "strengthen and balance" the muscles that I still have and to perhaps regain some of the muscle strength that I have already lost.

Christina, my young therapist, greeted me and informed me right after our introduction and her assessment of my skills that this therapy was going to be difficult for me. Apparently, my current level of weakness was worse than I thought it was. She continued with further initial testing skills. I was horrified! My right side, also my dominant side, was apparently losing the battle but hopefully not the war. Maybe with Christine's guidance, I can regain some muscle loss. It will, as she explains, be hard work. She went on with her assessment. "Don't let me pull this, push this as hard as you can." She instructed me to do some additional exercises and told me that I could rest for five minutes if and when I got tired. I needed a rest five minutes into the first exercise.

Finally, this very long day is coming to a close. My body is tired, and I am having a difficult time listening to the conversations swirling around in my head. There is so much happening at the same time. I try to focus on the more important one: selling my home and not risk going up and down the steps and breaking a hip or my arm. The obvious next important task that needs to be focused on is the community and one-level home where we will next reside.

I am tired and concerned about my health. Will any of this affect my balance, my vision, and my right side? I do not think so because it is all for the better and an all-new environment. Once I get over the sadness of leaving my woods, friends, and neighbors, I know it will all be fine. My body has to take this opportunity and begin to calm down and relax more. It is clear that stress exacerbates any Multiple Sclerosis condition.

Wednesday, March 26

This morning I woke up thinking about life when I was still teaching versus life these days, not teaching. In the past, I would have had to take a shower last night, prepare my lunch and diet snacks, search to find an outfit suitable for work, and check and recheck to be certain that I had my already fully charged cell phone. I lie here in bed wondering how I managed to do it all plus teach a whole day. I guess you do what you need to do when there is no other choice. My response to all of the questions concerning my health was always the same: "I am peachy."

At this very moment, I have an upbeat outlook. I have been part of a study group for MS through my world-renowned neurologist. I am scheduled to see him in a few days. Both of my neurologists work as a team and usually make joint decisions concerning my treatment. Together, they will decide my next course of action.

However, as I have already stated, I have read and researched as much as possible. Secondary Progressive MS does not have a set medical plan to prevent its progression. The only possible treatments have tremendous side effects without any guarantee that it will truly help to slow down progression. My primary neurologist feels that being on something is better than being on nothing. I have been on something that caused major life-altering side effects. I, therefore, am not of the mind-set that being on something is better than being on nothing. Perhaps one needs to experience the feeling of being run over by a truck before making such a statement. For me anyway, it has come down to quality of life.

Earlier in my day, I was feeling fairly well with a positive outlook. This afternoon was my third physical therapy session. I went into it feeling positive. Midway through, it became more and more difficult until it became impossible for me to do any of it. It was reaffirmed today that my right side—hand, leg, arm, all of it—is definitely weaker than my left side. Just that thought alone scares the life out of me. I am sure I need physical therapy, but I am not sure that I can. Today, I could barely walk out to my car. Thank goodness, the ride home was a mere six minutes. I crawled up the steps on all fours, crawled to my bed, and could not do one more thing.

Soon, the rest of the world will be eating dinner. Soon, I hope to be sleeping, that is the only way I will not continue to feel this excruciating pain.

Friday, March 27

Yesterday was a blur. I do not think I was able to concentrate, walk, and stand but slept for many hours. I was unable able to even think about the files, phone calls and accomplished nothing.

Today, I have a dentist appointment for a cleaning. I get my teeth cleaned twice a year and very rarely have a cavity. My gums have been shrinking right along with the rest of me. I take a large one-shot amount of antibiotics one hour before my appointment. My dentist's theory is to attack my immune system before it attacks me. My shrinking gums bleed profusely these days, with the cleaning, and even when I brush my teeth. My anemic smile shouts out to the world that I am sick. Multiple Sclerosis affects every bodily function! I am tired. There are many expletives I can use to describe my pain. In summary, I am just tired and weary.

Saturday, March 29

We went to see our friend in the hospital. On the surface, it appears, for the past forty-eight hours anyway, his medications have helped. Time will tell. Our friend has been through some difficult times. The death of his wife was shocking and sudden. It is difficult to see him so shattered and so very frightened. Before he lost his wife, he appeared to be so strong and so sure of himself. Now, without confidence, he is prone to anxiety attacks. His panic attacks have taken over who and what he was. His only chance is to try and rebuild himself, by himself and for himself. He has a tough road ahead.

After our visit with him today, I began to wonder what the hospital was going to do for him once he is released. Without life skills, without some tools to assist him with his new life, he will be released, will struggle to make it on his own, fail, and be right back in the hospital again, still depressed and still lost. That is my prediction. I feel he needs long-term survival skills, not short-term fixes. Our economy is in crisis and my friend works for a commercial contractor. They are a company that builds hospitals and other commercial buildings. Our president just had to bail out the banks; how many of them are going to continue with any commercial lending? I feel sooner than later, his job will be at risk.

Our other friend is dealing with his wife's sudden bone cancer and her rapidly climbing markers. He is another one whose future is uncertain. What are his options? How can we help him? He and my husband are life-long friends. He will be right there to support his friend. We both will. That is if I can, if I am able to.

Today was a day of reckoning and realizations. Each one of us have everyday feelings and struggles that are right there, front and center, in all of our lives. The only difference is the degree in which our personal issues are allowed to affect our individual lives. Unfortunately, no one is indomitable; we are all vulnerable. Anything can happen at any time. In a moment, in an instance, our lives could change. Win the lottery, and it changes for the better. As that last number is read and it matches the one on your ticket, your life is, to whatever degree, about to change. If I should fall the wrong way and break a bone, my daily life, as I know it now, would be even more difficult than it currently is. The difference is attitude, and outlook. We all know it is true, positive outlook, blah, blah, blah—some days it simply just takes too much energy to be positive.

Sunday, March 30

Today is Easter Sunday. We have been invited to dinner at my sister-in-law's family home. She and I have a pleasant relationship and I happily accepted her invitation. She and her husband are also going through their own problems. I was sworn to secrecy and promised not to repeat her secret. Sadly, she was diagnosed with breast cancer, will soon undergo surgery to remove her breast. She will eventually have reconstructive surgery. Her news only reaffirmed my prior conversations. Everyone has mountains to climb and obstacles that must be endured. Attitudes make the difference. Everyone possesses safety mechanisms, those defenses kick into action and it is those defenses that allows each person the ability to handle a tragedy. How we cope with it or to deal with our own difficulties is paramount to their outcomes. This case will be an ongoing story until her reconstruction is complete. Hopefully, that will be the end of her tragic saga, and hopefully, she truly will be cancer free for the rest of her life.

My heart hurts for her, but I look at her story as a successful one. Her future depends on the answer to one question: can she remain cancer free? If she can, her story is bright.

When I look at my own story and peer into my future, I don't see it as a bright one. I fear that my future is grim. There is no surgery to remove MS. MS is progressive and incurable. End of story.

Monday, March 31

Easter Day was pleasant, full of laughter and food. I cannot believe how much I ate. The day went well.

My nephew informed me that he has yet to RSVP to his invitation for my retirement party this Friday. My brother and sister-in-law have yet to respond also. Apparently, he was having some difficulty rescheduling some business appointments. He knows how important this is to me and how difficult my forced retirement is. He will be there.

I heard from the teacher organizing the party, and she informed me that she was surprised as to how many of my colleagues have responded positively. I was not. I already knew that I worked side by side with very special people. As I fell asleep, I remember thinking one last thought. I should begin to put together my "Thank You" speech. I tell myself to stop the internal conversation and go to sleep.

Tuesday, April 2

Today was another exhausting and relentless day of physical therapy, another crippling and numbing ninety minutes. My right leg was deadweight. Walking to my car was extremely difficult. I do not understand the concept of physical therapy and pushing myself to the point of falling and losing control over my muscles. How much is too much and how much will help me? My gut tells me that I should not be doing this much; my mind tells me that toning, stretching, and strengthening *has* to be done. I have always heard the expression, "Go with your gut instinct!" Can that expression apply to PT, please? My gut is telling me to stop. Therapy hurts and exhausts me, and I want to stop!

Sunday, April 5

It is Sunday morning, and this is my first chance to stop and ponder this very busy weekend. My "retirement party" was on Friday night. Everyone that I hoped would be there was. My stepdaughter and her fiancé came up from Virginia/DC for the party and stayed for the remainder of the weekend. On Saturday, we were having a wedding-planning meeting to go over details of the what, when, and where detailing different aspects of her big day. Her wedding date was getting closer and there were still so many open-ended items that needed attention from her "to do" list.

I have had very little success until now in being able to prevent or even understand my Multiple Sclerosis attacks and those terrible and horrifying paralyzing episodes. Unfortunately, on Friday, the day of my retirement dinner, it happened. Now, one can conjecture that Friday would have been a day that I was looking forward to. All of my colleagues and my family were there, and I had the opportunity to spend time with all of them together for a wonderful evening. I remained in my bed, resting most of the day in preparation for the evening's events. My body was feeling the aftermath from PT earlier in the week but, certainly, not enough to cripple my evening.

Unbelievably, by it was time to shower and dress, I could not walk, or talk, or even sit up from my prone position! I called for my husband. I was horrified. Both of my legs had that "cemented to the floor" feeling, and the rest of my right side was completely inoperable. Each time I tried to stand, I fell; and when I sat, I fell over to one side.

My husband was quite upset as the minutes turned into an hour and a half. It was time to leave, and I was going downhill quickly. My right hand was limp and clearly not listening to my brain as it gave clear instructions. It was time to put on panty hose, usually a very easy request. I am a middle-aged woman and must have successfully completed the panty hose maneuver hundreds of times.

My husband, who by now was beyond hysterical, could not assist in the panty hose fiasco, and decided that we needed assistance with this very difficult motion, He shouted to his daughter to come into the bedroom. Now stop for a moment. Try to imagine three people trying to put on one pair of panty hose on someone. Three people attempting such a ridiculous maneuver was a foolish notion. The worst part of it was that I could not sit up long enough to accomplish this very difficult task. I was dripping in sweat, my husband was shouting and announcing the time, and my stepdaughter was telling my husband that his hysteria was doing more harm than good. I was close to tears during the entire fiasco.

Now, in hindsight, the panty hose story will always remain somewhere in the crevices of our brain as one of the most ridiculous family moments that families can share. If you can picture two people attempting to dress a mannequin, from the undergarments to the outer garment, there is nothing left to do but laugh. Of course, the giggles came long after the game of beat the clock!

The next simple task to accomplish was getting me down our flight of steps to the bottom level and out to the car. I had absolutely *no* feeling and could not stand. More time was passing. Finally, with little option, my step-son picked me right up, carried me to the car, put me in the front seat, fastened my seat belt, and off we went.

As we drove to the party, we all wondered why we put ourselves through the exhausting panty hose attempt. I had many possibilities in terms of clothes. Why didn't we just switch from a dress to a pant outfit?

When we got to the retirement venue hall, they carefully placed me into my wheelchair. My husband gathered my nephews and stepson together. My grand entrance into my party was yours truly being carried by four men down a short flight of stairs while sitting in my wheelchair. They actually carried the chair with me still in it. I was mortified! My entrance scene was comparable to a queen being carried in on her throne.

Everyone was watching as I entered. Every one, both colleagues and family, gasped as I made my grand entrance into the ballroom. I watched their facial expressions, they were aghast at my deteriorated condition. My colleagues had not seen me in months and were visibly shaken that I was not able to walk in on my own. My family was saddened because they knew that for me to have to be carried in and not be able walk in on my own was both devastating and demoralizing for me. They were all correct in their thinking. I am a proud person. If there was one place, at one time, that I did not want a scene, it would have been that night.

The evening was fun; I was happy to see everyone all together and in one place. The numbness subsided enough for me to have a good time. However, I did not get out of my chair, and when I did, it was only to go to the ladies' room, and I had plenty of escorts to keep me out of harm's way. Understanding my predicament, people came to my table throughout the evening to extend their "Best of Luck in Retirement" wishes. For me, that evening was "the Best of Times and the Worst of Times." Truer words were never spoken.

Sunday, April 13

Today is Misty's birthday. She is just three years old. I selected her out of a liter of four Shih Tzu puppies from a breeder. She was only 5 weeks old. I picked her up the Sunday in June after the school year ended. The weeks between choosing which puppy out of the liter and bringing her home was time that she still needed to be weaned by her mom. Misty has been trained as my service dog, she has a federal identification tag and she is with me all of the time. I honestly could not imagine life without her.

Thursday, April 24

I am into the second phase of my injection therapy. I feel weak and sick in the mornings, but by midday, the side effects begin to slowly subside. My weakness and balance improves for a few hours, and I feel like I can handle this illness, it's not so bad. Unfortunately, reality sets in as I become so weak and tired and find it so very difficult to function. I try so very hard not to give into this illness, but truth be told—I say this once again—MS is larger and bigger than I am.

I can substantiate that fact. There are times, many times, that I have fallen and do not have enough strength to get myself up again. Yes, those are the times that I have had to realize, quietly, that MS and I are in conflict. Sooner or later, I will lose, my disease will keep me on the floor most of the time. The moments I can get up on my own are becoming less and less. Sooner or later, I will be defeated and MS will win.

My husband is finding his role as a "caretaker" difficult. He tries to maintain his composure and is considerate and understanding. There are times he loses his patience and raises his voice in frustration. Can you recall a time when you found yourself in a conversation with someone who does not speak your language? Do you remember raising your voice as you were talking? Think back to that time; they did not understand your words as you spoke to them in a regular-conversation voice, so why did you think they would understand those same words in a louder, almost shouting voice?

My husband does that very same action. He says something to me, and when my body does not respond, he shouts. Why does he think my body would respond to a louder voice if it didn't respond to his conversational voice? It's so ridiculous that you have to chuckle. Not really, but a little levity never hurt anyone.

He is shouting because he is also very scared and he is one person doing the work of two. He is loud because he is doing everything from food shopping to laundry. A caretaker's role is a difficult one. He has to watch his wife becoming less and less able to ambulate. He can't make my disease go away, and as my husband, he just wants to fix me and bring both of our lives back to what they once were. Slowly but surely, he is coming to realize that he cannot. Therein lies his fear.

It is very difficult, for anyone, any couple, and any family, to suddenly have to alter the course of their life. We did not have prior knowledge and were unaware of the ramifications that such a major illness could deliver. Any family who has had to endure any abrupt and unexpected illness will understand.

Just take one little step at a time, take a deep breath, look at the bright side (there always is one), stand tall, and stay together. You will see, the rest will somehow just fall in place. Just believe in yourself.

Monday, May 5

I have had a lower-back problem since my college days. My friend and I became involved in horseback riding. There was nothing as soothing as a ride through the wooded trails. It was almost therapeutic. I could be mindless yet full of thoughts at the same time, resulting in an hour of tranquility.

My dad introduced me to horseback riding. I do not remember how old I was; I only remember that being so high off the ground terrified me.

On this particular day, I had difficulty switching from a Western galloping position to the rhythm of a cantor ride. My horse became frightened and began running. I was not able to move with him in a cantor rhythm. The muscles in my lower back were injured and sprained. Still today, whenever I sit too long, it is uncomfortable. The treatment for my lower back involves a combination of ice and heat therapy. It does not take long before I begin to feel pain free.

Thursday, May 8

I woke up this morning with what appeared to be a huge boil on my lower left back and hip area. It felt like there was a hot iron just sitting on the spot. I went into the bathroom (isn't that something we all have to do the first thing in the morning?). I lifted up my nightshirt. I felt so weak with pain and was compelled to discover the source. I found a large boil-like object. The skin surrounding this large sac of liquid was fire engine red.

Once I realized the severity of the site, I shouted for my husband. It took both of us to realize that it was a burn. We tried to use gauze and some Band-Aids to cover it up. It was similar to a balloon waiting to be popped. It hurt so badly. We tried to be so careful not to touch it. I was able to wear loose clothing. My husband helped me into my car. It felt as though someone was holding a hot iron to my body.

I immediately drove to my primary care doctor. He examined me and concluded that I had a third degree burn. He strongly suggested that I see my Dermatologist as soon as possible. I left the doctor's office, sat in my car, and located Dr. Dermatologist's office number in my cell phone. His first available appointment to see me was on Monday, May 15. I had a third degree burn diagnosed by my Primary Care Doctor!

I was in excruciating pain, how could I wait until Monday? I am sure I will have to use the pain pills that were prescribed. I usually do not take pain pills, but I can feel this burning was severe, constant, and consistent.

Once I was able to determine what happened, it all made sense. The heating pad I used last night, manufactured by a large lawless Corporation and imported from China, was the cause of my severe burn.

I quickly discovered that this Company's prior actions or inactions to be unconscionable. In my case, the timer never shut off as it was designed, advertised, and marketed. It *did not*, I repeat, did not shut off. The automatic shutoff failed! How could I have known that the timer could fail while the heating pad continued to remain on for an indeterminate amount of time?

I became angry, I was going through these painful treatments at Dr. Dermatologist's office and was never given a warning of that possibility. Stop for a minute and think about what I am saying. It was unbelievable! The heating pad remained on and never shut off! I fell asleep! I woke up in the morning to find this huge burn. I contacted the manufacturer to inform them of what was happening.

The company denied any wrongdoing; simply put, they should be ashamed of themselves in not prewarning the consumers. Money does not make the world go round; humanity, kindness, and a sense of self do make the world go round. Everyone knows that, except the large companies. Why wasn't I informed?

I slept most of that upcoming weekend. When I wasn't sleeping, I could feel the pain. I should have been warned!

Monday, May 12

I saw Dr. Dermatologist today. He took pictures and agreed that my wound was a third-degree burn and asked how it happened. I told him the same story about the heating pad failing. He informed me that the process he would begin today would take months and leave a permanent scar. He began treatments after he numbed the area.

It took several hours and I bled profusely. I did not realize the degree of the injury. There was no way I could drive home. I had to call my husband and my son to pick me up. They drove together in one car so that I could go home with my husband and my son could drive my car home.

I was exhausted and collapsed into my bed the minute I got home. I remained there for the remainder of the day and for the next few days as well.

Thursday, May 15

I was able to see Dr. Dermatologist. He performed another treatment to the site wound. Yet again, I face more debreeding and endless bleeding. I had never experienced this kind of pain. The "hot iron" feeling never seems to subside.

Tonight is a major school event and I would have been a Presenter. It is Student Achievement Awards and it is quite an accomplishment for the students. I would not be able to attend, and not be able to hug my achievers. I am quite disappointed. They will miss me too.

Why wasn't Mary Q. Public informed that the timer could malfunction while the heating pad functioned, causing my third-degree burn?

What could I say?

Friday, May 16

Fatigued, physical therapy, fatigued, Dr. Dermatologist, fatigued, home, bed, and sleep. For me, it is just one more pain-enduring day.

Monday, May 19

Today is my wedding anniversary. The number of years is unimportant. My Godparents celebrated their fiftieth wedding anniversary and that was quite a celebration. This year the four of us celebrated together. We spent a few hours together and it was fun reminiscing. My Godparents have always been there to "cover my back," even when I did not think it needed covering. If they thought I needed anything, they were there. I am proud to spend this special day with two of my favorite people.

Saturday, May 24

I thought that I would spend the whole afternoon working on paperwork. I file them chronologically so I can keep tight tabs on the next file. There are so many incomplete projects, moving, selling, and buying, and it goes on and on.

I began the day with breakfast with my husband. It was 5:15 AM and a dark morning. Once he left, my intention was to return to my bed up one flight of steps. The truth is, he left, and just like that, with no warning and no reason, I fell on the hard ceramic floor. I was suddenly numb and could not get off of the floor for quite a few hours. I just did not have enough strength. I cried doing the shimmy dance on all fours on my belly. In other words, I crawled in the direction of the staircase. I could not muster up enough energy to go up one step at a time. Whenever I attempted to get up, I would fall back down again. Unfortunately the second fall was always harder because my body and muscle strength were already exhausted from my fall only 5 seconds earlier . . .

On a few of the failed attempts to stand, I hit my head on the hard ceramic-tile kitchen floor. My emergency "help me" buttons were all on my nightstand, beside my bed, on the second floor! Remember, I only came down to have a cup of coffee with my husband. Neither one of us thought that I was so weak that I could not pick myself off of the floor or even get up to my bedroom.

Multiple Sclerosis is a very unpredictable annoyance to my everyday life.

My body is feeling this sore from so many falls. These past few weeks have left me feeling worse. The falls are increasing and my balance is decreasing. Why? The nighttime pain is horrible. My bones hurt. The pain is so intense and awakens me. There is no medication that helps alleviate the intensity. Once I am awake with the pain, I cannot fall back to sleep. The following day, I am physically and emotionally drained. Tomorrow, my husband will need to stay home with me. I will not be able to be left alone. Is this a result of the stress from the burn?

Could it be?

Monday, June 9

My husband and I attended my last retirement dinner last night at the perfect venue, a district favorite restaurant. It was absolutely fantastic! The food was excellent. The meal began with a delicious appetizer, an open bar, and ended with a delicious dessert display. The evening was bittersweet for me. It was wonderful to celebrate with my colleagues, a comfortable and relaxing evening; but it really marked another step toward the "retirement" world and leaving this life and, for the most part, most of these people behind. I will miss the sharing.

My birthday is in a few days. I am not excited nor am I apathetic about it. At my age, it really is just another day. Birthdays from now on will mark another year of the questionable walking to nonwalking or still feeling or being numb. I do, however, celebrate every year that I still can do what I may not be able to do tomorrow. We all should enjoy the time today whether we have a disease or not. Here is an example: I am grateful for my body tolerating Betaseron. Perhaps my body is developing an immunity to it, perhaps this and perhaps that. Don't project or look to the future; deal with today. Who the hell knows what tomorrow may bring?

Tuesday, June 10

My brother and sister-in-law have been married for close to thirty years. They have four children who have all had birthday parties, graduation parties, and the like. Therefore, for decades, there have been many occasions for celebrations at their home. Both sides of the family were always there for the children. The kids are grown. My sister-in-law's mom has also attended these same celebrations.

We all have grown older together and have become one large extended family. My sister-in-law's mom has grown older graciously. She is in her eighties now and is suffering with diabetes. She has endured surgery after surgery and has always stood proud and tall. She is a dedicated grandma and all of her grandchildren have enjoyed the relationship with grandma. She is a dedicated grandma and would never consider missing any of her grandchildren's celebrations.

She and I have a common bond—we both suffer with different diseases, both diseases simply put, would suck the life out of anyone. Our conversations usually focus on our everyday difficulties in doing this or that. As I have tried to explain, those that are afflicted have a different version of the same story. The story is one that begins on the inside and the fright that is usually not explain to others.

Recently, she experienced a fear when she fell in her home in the middle of the night. She was lodged as she landed between her sink and her toilet. She broke her neck in four different places, and the emergency squad had a difficult time pulling her out of a very tiny corner. They had to get her head tightly secured with no chance of it dislodging on a board designed for those unfortunate enough to sustain such a critical injury. She is in an adult rehabilitation center and can never live alone again.

I share this story for many reasons. The primary reason to tell her story is to share with you the anguish and dilemma that the elderly and disabled endure. This is the United States of America. We provide for the world, why aren't we extending much needed resources for large population of the elderly? As a nation, we are proud of our new and modern medical breakthroughs and new drug discoveries that keep Mom around longer. The only problem herein lies with finances. I know of quite a few families that are concerned about health care coverage. Unfortunately, I am sure you do too. Yes, Mom is here, but where do we get the dollars necessary to provide and care for her? There is a lot of conversation these days about our health-care coverage. Maybe that coverage could provide just a tiny more for our elderly and our disabled. As I have said many times before, "Let's first take care of our own."

Sunday, June 15, Father's Day

My stepfather passed away a few years back. My biological dad is alive and well but has no contact with his children. That is fine for me. My outlook is a simple one, and it is his loss. Case closed; end of story.

I went to the cemetery to say hello to my stepfather. He resides in a mausoleum. I thought about the idea of "visiting him." We sit on a bench in front of a wall divided in to parts. Each partition had another name carved into it. I wanted to tell him that I missed him. But then I wondered, Why am I sitting on a bench and talking to a wall? I continued to tell him what was new and how the family was doing. I remained on that bench just long enough for my inner voice to start up. I knew then that it was time to leave. I could have and will speak to him more often without looking at his name engraved into stone. Either way, I do miss him though.

Sunday, June 22

It is one day after we listed our home for sale. We have been preparing to open our home to prospective buyers. Some items were thrown away, other items were given away, and other items were donated. We have, as they say, "lightened our load." Along those same lines, we also listed our summer property for sale. The real estate market has taken a nosedive and has fallen into a downward spiral. We will just have to play the wait-and-see game

On another note, the wife of my husband's best friend continues to receive bad news with regard to her health. She has been diagnosed with bone cancer. She had breast cancer some years back. The cancer is spreading quickly now, and she is on antihormonal therapy. Her husband and my husband have been best friends for over thirty years. It is heart wrenching to talk with her. She is a nurse who understands what is happening to her and how much time she has left to live. She is a mom with four children. There is no need to go further than that one sentence.

She and I were able to have a heart-to-heart conversation. One in which we can both discuss what the end of our lives will be. We hugged each other as we openly talked about the end of our lives and how much pain we will have to endure. We cried together as we discussed our ending and the impact it will have on those we leave behind. Neither of us could bring our husbands or children into the conversation. We could not bring ourselves to picture their faces as we took our last breath.

Our final bear hug spoke volumes without having uttered a word. I am certain that her inner conversations torment her too.

On a positive note, I have a contract of sale for our beautiful home in front of me. A few nights ago, around 7:00 PM, a couple rang our front doorbell. They had been looking for a home in our development and saw our For Sale sign. Both their attorney and ours have been in contact, and a price has been agreed on. I have prequalified them for a mortgage, and they have enough money and job security to obtain a mortgage. Their credit is fine. We will sign this contract. Our next step is to go back to the house we fell in love with and make an offer to purchase.

We are undergoing life's major stress moments. I have to be as calm as I can so all of this does not bring me into an exacerbation attack. Once we can secure our new home, the rest of the upcoming days will be easier.

As all of this occurs, my burn site is undergoing mini surgeries to debreed the site. It is very painful, and if anything brings me down, it will be the Corporation and the heating pad that burned me without providing a consumer warning.

Monday, June 23

School is over for this year. Another year has passed. Burn treatments continue. Selling our home, buying a home with only one level, no stairs, packing, moving, falling, and falling some more.

Friday, July 11

This past week was nerve shattering. It is imperative that our buy contract and our sell contract close on the same day. We need the money from the first home to buy the second. Rich we are not.

Soon, we are going to meet our daughter at the beach. She and her husband will drive north and we will meet for breakfast; from there we will do the beach thing. I am so worried about it. What if it is a humid day? My illness prevents me from doing the "oven" baking anymore. I remember the days that my cousin and I used to go to the beach and use pure baby oil to tan. Today, people used skin protector number 30 to prevent skin cancer.

Here is a thought; maybe someday Multiple Sclerosis will have a cure and injection therapy will also be something that people did in the days of yesteryear. I am certain I have had this thought before.

My inner conversation could just go on and on. Always questioning the "what if" and "why me." For now, however, my mind must get back to the day we meet our daughter on the beach and how I will survive my MS and any side effects from the heat.

Saturday, July 12

The weather outside was warm; no humidity, and a clear blue sky. There was even a breeze off of the ocean. My husband and I were only on the beach for a few minutes. We were still drinking our coffee and had not put up our umbrella yet. It had been only been partly sunny before they arrived. Consequently, we both felt no urgency to provide shade for me.

We were talking and having a great time together. Suddenly and without warning, I lost all muscle control. My husband had been quietly observing my movements, looking for any signs of trouble. He saw the beginning stages and came over to try to lift me. I was in "rag doll" mode, making it impossible to lift me. It was as if he was lifting one thousand pounds.

The worse I became, the more worried and nervous I was. Because I was nervous, I became even more worried. It was becoming a vicious circle. We needed to do whatever we could to avert this attack and, hopefully, before the kids arrived. First, he put the umbrella up, which put me in the shade. Next, he went to the showers and filled containers with water. By the time he was done with his back-and-forth trips—filling the container, coming back to me, pouring the water contents over me, and rushing back to get more water—which he made fifteen times, I was as wet as if I had just taken a shower. I still had no control over any part of my body.

When our daughter arrived, she asked me how the water was. She assumed I was wet because I had been in the ocean. We did not tell her that going in the ocean and being beat up by the waves was an activity that I could no longer do. She did not realize that her father was not wet; therefore, nothing else was said.

Two hours later, I could feel the attack lifting. The breeze kicked up and I kept on trying to lift my legs. I started feeling better and needed to use the ladies' room. It was up three flights of concrete steps. Again, I was fearful that I could do it without falling or making a scene. My daughter and I walked there together. She did not suspect anything.

We did everything we could today to have a leisurely and fun family day. It looks like we pulled it off today, but my internal fears never stop. What about the next attack? Where will I be? Will I be able to stop it? My fear of tomorrow continues. Why didn't we scout out the beach and search for one where the ladies' room was not so far away? What were we thinking?

It is true what they say. I really do not accept or acknowledge this disease. Someday, I will find myself in a predicament that I will not be able to escape from. How does that saying go? Everyone knows it. It talks about having courage and "accepting those things I cannot change."

Easier said than done.

Tuesday, July 15

I have completed our mortgage application package and included all of the necessary supporting documentation. There is one home that my husband has fallen in love with. It has an "open floor" plan, which would be the best for me in my electric wheelchair. Of course, it is the most expensive. I made an offer considerably lower than the asking price. We are excellent purchasers, and that fact alone is why the sellers should accept our offer.

This morning's newspaper, on the front page, in big bold print, the following words appeared: "Mortgage Giants See Stock Slide Despite Help." Banks will be particular when approving mortgages. That is the reason I spent so much time on it. I am not concerned about our approval; my concern is the timing of both the buy and the sell and my buyers getting their mortgage commitment in and around the same time. The newspaper article also included the following phraseology: "Waning Confidence Sends Banking Industry Stocks Slumping."

It is certainly not the best housing market in terms of sales, and definitely not the best time for mortgage approvals. Again, my mind quickly goes to my buyer and his ability to obtain a mortgage approval. He was when I prequalified him, but it appears that the banking industry is apprehensive with regard to lending. I will be nervous now about our buyers getting approval for a mortgage.

I am almost finished with treatments for my burn. It has been a few months of pain and appears to be a permanent scar. The scar is secondary to the fact that my MS has taken a ride on the one-way Southbound Express. Once you are on this train, there is no turning back and no getting off. You have lost control over your own destiny.

Sunday, July 20

My bones hurt so very badly. I feel muscle soreness. I can't think straight, and details are all foggy. Sometimes, I can't remember the simplest name. For instance, I could not recall the name of the town I used to live in. I did not want anyone to know of my mental lapse. I frantically and discreetly searched around for some clue that would help me to recall whatever it was that I couldn't remember.

Lately, this is happening a lot. It is frightening when you are unable to recall an item mentioned only ten minutes earlier. I will have to make an appointment to see my neurologist, and I will tell him all of this. Most of it, however, is clearly written on my face. I try to hide my pain, but this time, I am afraid that it is obvious. I am unable to walk more than a few steps without falling.

Monday, July 21

When I explained to the receptionist at my neurologist's office how I was feeling, she put me on hold for what seemed like less than a minute. She was back quickly to tell me that I needed to get to him today. I reminded her that we had moved and were an hour away. Her reply was short and sweet: "If not today, then first thing tomorrow morning." The tone of her voice in combination with her message carried a flavor of urgency. I did not understand why, but I complied with her instructions. An appointment time was scheduled for the following morning.

I am happy with my new injections of Betaseron. I *do* have side effects, so please do not start jumping up and down and shouting. Everything I take has side effects. When I say I am happy with Betaseron, I refer only to being able to tolerate the drug. My body and Rebif could not cohabit. I was very sick from the drug itself. The side effects were disastrous, and without question the drug "put me down," "took me out"—whatever analysis one chooses to use is fine. The major point here is that, comparatively speaking, my body tolerated one drug and onstead another medication injection savagely poisoned my body.

Tuesday, July 22

Both my tri level town home where I currently live and my future home are in contract. It has all happened so quickly. We are waiting for both lenders to approve the mortgages, our mortgage to purchase and our buyers' mortgage to purchase our home. It is scary because it comes down to "the domino theory." If one piece of this puzzle fails, the entire project will fail and we will have to find another buyer or simply stay put. Since the steps are a major problem just waiting to happen, finding a second potential buyer will take some time. As I have stated, it all comes down to our buyer obtaining an approval for their mortgage to purchase our home.

My neurologist appointment did not go well for me. In my heart, I have known that I was experiencing an exacerbation of my MS, but there is so much going on at this time. I honestly felt that there was very little time for me to be any sicker or doing any less than I was doing. If my declination continues as this pace, my caretaker will need a caretaker. He probably could use one now.

In the next few days, a nurse will come to my home and put a port into my arm. She will stay until the first bag empties so that she could monitor my vitals. There is always a concern that my body could have a reaction to the medication. I had no adversity, but she stayed for the hour that it took for the first bag to empty. My husband and I will have to set up the second and third bags of medication. Again, each bag will take an hour to empty. He recommended these same three days of bed rest. This round of treatment, intravenous, at home, is the last attempt to curtail this round of heightened systems. The next step involves a longer IV treatment in the hospital.

I will adhere to his warning and stay in bed as long as I can over these three days. Whatever has to be followed up on, I can do from my home. The primary piece of the puzzle, our buyer's mortgage commitment, once approved, will help to lessen the tension.

Wednesday, July 23

Whenever I stand and attempt to take a few steps, I fall. Once I am on the floor, I am unable to get up. Each time I try, I fall again. A second attempt leaves me sprawling all over the floor, unable to control my muscles. My lower back is exceptionally weak. I cannot sit up from a prone position on my own. I need something I can use to pull myself up, a sort of makeshift pulley. I had to press my alert button for emergency assistance.

My mother-in-law was rushed to the hospital an hour ago. She fell in her home; she is ninety-one and lives alone. For obvious reasons, her living by herself will no longer be an option. She pressed her medical alert button for the emergency squad. She will need a 24/7 live-in aide to continue to stay in her home.

For obvious reasons, I can no longer live alone and already have a 24/7 live-in caretaker, my husband. Without him, my mother-in-law and I are in the similar situations.

Our lives run parallel and our ages are decades apart. This is a notion that I choose not to ponder for more than a fleeting minute.

Friday, July 25

Today I had another appointment with my neurologist. These past few weeks have not been my best. I actually fell right in his inner office today and that fall occurred after my intravenous treatment. If I had to fall anywhere, it sure as hell would never be right in his office, knowing that his recommended treatment was for me to be in the hospital for a longer treatment of intravenous steroids to slow down this drastic exacerbation decline.

The doctor once again made an attempt for me to begin a monthly infusion of Tysabri. When my husband and I read the frightening side effects, I decided against taking the drug. He agreed. I have firsthand experienced life-threatening side effects of a drug my body rejected. I do not want to risk feeling that way again. It comes down to quality of life, and I would rather feel MS pain than the deadly effects of poison in my system.

My burn treatments continue. I have had months of pain and suffering and a feeling of anger for the company that burned me without warning. It is obvious, however, the corporate giants do nor care about the small time consumer.

Saturday, July 26

We talk about it, we think about it, we wonder, we worry, and we discuss it some more. Should I chance the monthly infusion? They have been making long strides in perfecting its usage and perhaps they have even reduced the risks, but will one monthly infusion for an hour of a chemotherapy type of medication kill me or help me? It can't make me better, the Secondary Progressive MS means exactly what it says, and the disease is progressive. I can't ever get better than I am. I will never get my balance back, my vision back, or my full cognitve ability to recall recent events. The drugs I have taken so far have already or soon will become ineffective because my body has or will develop antibodies to the drug.

I very rarely discuss my fears. I am petrified of losing my ability to feed myself, wipe myself, or even brush my teeth. My internal self is never quiet, is rarely settled, and if allowed, has the potential to overpower me. A medical professional has explained that there are no guarantees that anything can be done and all medication currently on the market is experimental. The proven drugs with any possibility of slowing down the disease may work on someone who has recently been diagnosed. My only hope is that I do not become paralyzed. Being completely paralyzed is a fate worse than death. It is clear that I need to avoid stress and listen to my body when it reminds me that I need to limit my activities. Once I am settled in a new home, I will make it my business to plan nonconcurrent functions. As a precaution, I might begin practicing to brush my teeth with my left, less dominant hand.

Sunday, July 27

My husband did his usual morning activity of running to the food store to buy food for the week. He needs his "salad ingredients" and he tries to go early before I wake up. After the food store, he will run into Wal-Mart to purchase large plastic containers. Once they are here, we can officially begin to pack. The garbage bags, step one, are finished for now. Together, we will go through different areas. It becomes simple: the items we are taking go into plastic containers. The items we are not taking, go into black garbage bags.

Some years back, we both said that we would never go through the exhausting process of moving. It is a beautiful day. I am writing this as I sit perched on my living room sofa, watching some deer, a turkey family, cardinals, and our usual robin's nest. This home is all I ever wanted, but the balance between beauty and safety has tilted. I am falling now more each day. It is time to go. Why do I have to? Why is my MS getting so bad? I know I must have written this question before because I repeat the same thoughts to myself over and over.

I am just about finished with the burn wound. A huge scar remains but additional surgery, for the sake of vanity, would not be a wise decision. The burn site tightens, pulls, and in those ways, always reminds me that it is there. Be careful of heating pads and their potential hazards. The manufacturer may not inform the public, so I will, little me, a no one.

Monday, July 29

Today I remembered an older song by Diana Ross. I searched iTunes and found it. "It's My Turn" and I listened to it quite a few times. It has more meaning to me now because my illness has caused my time to be at a premium. There are now restrictions on what I can do and when I can do it. How much longer will I be able to . . . ? I have paid my dues. *My* time is now. My husband deserves more. We will do while I still can. I cannot really believe how very sick I feel. There are these moments and frightening thoughts that encompass my inner self. There is always an awareness that I will lose the battle and be conquered. Maybe today,maybe 5 years, but the realistic version of my MS story is always the same. Perhaps I will be lucky, do I have five years, five weeks, five months or five days? I can only pray for more time to be functional, in the end, I am certain I will be defeated. Therein lies my constant inner turmoil and fear. When? How?

Tuesday, August 5

In a few short days, I have fallen many times, but two of them came close to an ambulance ride to the closest hospital. I have a major head injury. I fell right into a glass-and-marble end table in my living room. My head hit it hard as I was falling. I shouted out with pain; my left temple is swollen, black and blue, and very sore to the touch. The wound is one half finger up from my left eye. Once again, I was fortunate, I fell hard and very suddenly. It happened without warning. I was unable to break my fall. In a fleeting moment I was up and just as quickly, I was down. I can not predict where or when, I have little warning, if any at all.

The second scare came as I was entering the sliding glass door leading to the outside deck. One second I was standing up, and in a flash, my body went hurling into the glass door with such a deadweight force, the screen door was knocked right off of its hinges. My body fell onto the concrete patio pavers, and there I lay, unable to move or get up from the cold concrete. I am also black and blue from that fall. The concrete was cold and wet. As a result, I have cuts and scrapes on my hands, arms, elbows, basically wherever skin touched patio. It is not a pretty sight; picture the combination of a black-and-blue forehead with cuts and bruises all over me from my body hurl onto the concrete.Can you visualize my appearance? There is no question about it, I was in a fight and the other person won. Looks good, huh? Rocky Balboa has nothing on me!

Wednesday, August 6

Despite my bruised body and throbbing head, for a few hours anyway, I continued on the task of closet cleaning. It is very difficult because I have three different sizes of everything combined with the seasonal aspect, so there are three sizes of everything needed for four seasons; there is just never enough closet room. I will continue to cull through what seems to be an endless task. I could use more than one walk-in closet for two people. Either that, or I need to cut out a few seasons of the year or stay one size. I'll get back to you right after I finish this bag of M&M's.

Thursday, August 7

I have only one thought to share with you today. Never, ever, ever move! The packing and packing goes on and on and on. Everywhere I look, there is still more to do. No, I stand corrected, there is much, much more to do. That's it, nothing else to add. After this move, which I have been forced to do, I will in no way move again.

Try this little game. Just stand in one room, look around at everything but the furniture, that's the easy part. Are you looking at the pictures hanging, the window treatments, the lamps, and the knick-knacks? Now, imagine the things you are not seeing; they too, my friend, will need to be boxed! Endless.

Friday, August 8

Here I sit (sitting is good), working through those seven files that need to be massaged every day. There is the purchase, the sale, the disability files, and the other four, totaling seven transactions all happening simultaneously.

So far, so good, but I can leave nothing to chance. Juggling seven balls at the same time and having them all land in the right place is quite a feat. Not difficult, as long as they all get tickled each day.

Picture this, if I am not packing, I am falling; after falling, I need to lie down. Another day comes, I feel so sick, and I can't even begin any packing. Another day comes, I do some packing, massage some files, need to lie down. And so on and so on and so on . . . Do you think I will move ever again?

Saturday, August 9

It amazes me how uncomfortable people feel when they find out I have a diagnosis of Multiple Sclerosis. Approximately, ninety-five percent of the time they reply with words that usually go like this: "My so-and-so has MS, they've had it since so-and-so." Of course, curious me—forever seeking to hear of a miracle cure that has been found, one of which I know nothing about—asks, "How are they doing? How long have they had it?"

Sometimes, their response comes quickly, sometimes they are hesitant, and others try to just fluff it off. I guess their response is based on their level of closeness to me. If they are close and fear my reaction, their answer is usually guarded, revealing as little as possible to me. Their sentences usually begin with, "Well, you know, every case of MS is different." Their goal is to sound as if they were an authority on the matter, when their real agenda is to end this conversation as quickly as possible. They are just trying to shield me from the grim possibilities.

Today, a total stranger revealed to me that her stepmother has MS, also in her mid-fifties, and is now just totally bedridden. That was her response after finding out that I had it. That sentence, her quick response, has and will have me in fear again for a while.

My husband and I recently met another couple; the wife has MS, and he is having to retire to be her full-time caretaker. His new caretaker responsibility forced him to retire years earlier than they had planned. He did this upon hearing from one of those people who told him that his uncle became totally blind and died recently. He still informed him even after he found out that the man's wife had MS.

I wonder if these people later think about their answers describing those that they know with the disease and, perhaps, rethink their replies. One would hope so, but my belief is that they do not.

Sunday, August 10

Moving day is about to arrive and I will be grateful. I am feeling the aftershock of both falls. My head is still sore to the touch around my left temple and the back of my neck; actually my entire neck is now hurting with every slight move. The more I fall, the more I become afraid of breaking one of my most needed bones.

I will have to lie down now. I suddenly need a nap and feel extremely exhausted. In a few short hours, my oldest nephew and his fiancée are being surprised with their bridal shower. I hope to feel better when I wake up; I have to go to the bridal shower, regardless of how I feel.

Monday, August 11

It is the end of a very long day. I am always amazed when I listen to the different people's responses when they discover that I have MS.

My amazement continues, everyone knows someone who has MS. Is it more prevalent these days, or is it just that I am attuned more to those two little letters? Could it be true that I never heard of it before, that MS was never discussed in a conversation that I was involved in, or is it truly more prevalent now? Suddenly, within five days, MS seems to be the topic of conversation. Coincidence?

The conversation involved sharing my MS diagnosis. I do what I can to bring this conversation to an early close. This wedding shower is not the marathon for MS donations. This is a bridal shower. I continue to function but my internal voice began to ask me, "Why the hell am I trying so hard when the final out come, will be the same regardless of what I do? A demoralizing conversation, at best.

Tuesday, August 12

I did not sleep well last night. The words, "She is totally bedridden now and thirty-four years," kept repeating over and over in my head. Do people regret it when they comment so foolishly to a disabled person? Do they even understand how I may react or do they even care?

Each of us has different types of relationships in our lives. There are those people who are our lives, our inner circle; we live with them or speak with them a few times a day. They are our parents, our children, our closest and dearest friends and family. These people would do anything for us and would go to great lengths to protect us and shield us from harm. If and when a "bedridden" sort of reply was said in their presence, they would not have allowed time for me to ask any questions; they would have changed the subject or come right out and prevented the conversation from continuing.

Another type of close relationship is still family and friends, loyal and protective; we may not speak or see them for weeks, but they are always on our calendar. These people would have felt very uncomfortable with the "bedridden" conversation and might not have known how to halt it with such urgency as Mom or hubby.

Finally, there are the strangers who act like fools and are the same people who hurry to inform us proudly that they know or knew of someone with the same disease and idiotically notify the disabled of their impending doom. These are the group of people I choose to live without. I have categorized people and their reactions before. I know I must have, I just am so shocked each and every time with their various reactions.

Friday, August 15

Last night was my husband's big retirement party. Everyone that he wanted was there from the many offices and regions he had worked in the last thirty-seven years, four months, and ten days. He repeatedly and very proudly informed anyone and everyone that asked how long he had been employed with the State of New Jersey. He was so excited about his dinner and repeatedly insisted that I rest and relax during the day. He really wanted to enjoy his evening without any MS episodes. I so wanted that for him as well. Consequently, I rested and rested some more.

The evening went fairly well. I tried to stay seated and still socialize, always very conscious of my appearance and any slurring in my speaking. My husband was happy. Both of our children were there, and he was very proud. It was a delightful evening until we arrived back home.

My son held on to me throughout the night and continued when we arrived back home. We drove into our parking lot, and my husband let me and my son out close to our entrance door.

My son held on to me as I carefully got out of the car. He let go of me for four seconds, just long enough to close the car door. In what felt like a flash, I fell onto the granite parking lot and hit my head hard enough for it to begin to bleed. My son literally picked me up off the ground and carried me into the kitchen.

I just laid my head into my folded arms on the kitchen table. I was so humiliated and ashamed. I tried so hard for this evening to be only about my husband, for him to have his evening with coworkers, friends, and family. He asked for it to just be for him, and now, here I lay, with a bloodied body and wounded head. Once again, an evening for him and about him ended up so very poorly.

Both men continued with their hysteria as they rummaged through my hair searching for the source of the blood, all in an attempt to discover the wound and decide if I needed to go to the hospital for stitches. My humiliation continued. The ice pack came out of the freezer and was placed on the wound.

After what felt like an eternity, they decided that I did not need to go to the emergency room and carried me up the steps to my bed. I could hear them both grunting as they left the bedroom. The words *denial, stubborn,* and *proud* resonated as they exited the bedroom. Usually, I may have accepted their words of doubt about my behavior in the future but for now, I demurred and prayed that I would fall asleep. I cried because I never imagined the last third of my life would end in heartache as well as such physical pain. My inner voice did all that it could in an attempt to console myself. Sometimes, most times, my pain over took my internal attempts of any sort of consolation.

It is moments such as these that prompted me to write down the horrifying consequences of this disease. I am sure your will agree that having a head concussion was not part of the evening agenda and I am sure that you will even agree that it was embarrassing. Now, picture yourself on the pavement in an evening dress waiting to be helped up from the damp ground. This Kodak Moment is not about denial or acceptance. I have no control over this frightening life sentence. These sudden body crashes carry no warning, in an instant I am down. I cannot predict when, where, how or why. Is it because I am tired? Nervous? It is a sudden loss of balance. These sudden moment to moment falls frighten everyone around me. I appear to stagger and sway, my body almost took on an undulating appearance. I have not yet accepted my fear of the unknown. I have no control over this disease, not in this Secondary Progressive Phase. Therefore, I understand the concerns of those around me.

Saturday, August 16

There was no question or doubt that my husband was visibly upset with me this morning, He was distant, and our desultory conversations were understandable to me. I knew the answer, but I urged him to vocalize exactly what he was feeling. I knew he was distressed. I stole his thunder! This one night should have been about him, in our home, laughing with the kids about this or that. It was ruined with emergency-room conversation.

I feel so very sorry. I was nervous when it was happening which I am sure made it that much worse. Everyone in my life wants me to see someone about my stubbornness and not accepting help. What kind of help would they like me to seek? How could I have prevented that fall? In just a few seconds I was down. I did not move an inch off the mark where he positioned me. My body was tired; it was an eventful and stressful day. How can I be held responsible for those frightening episodes?

Do you remember my fall in the school parking lot? Can you understand the humiliation I experienced as a result of that tumble? This fall resulted in a bleeding head wound, and the embarrassment of being carried up a flight of steps by an adult child.

I continue to have quiet moments with my inner self and that annoying little voice that never shuts up. There remain filled boxes and empty cartons strewn all around my bedroom. I am in the process of moving and am surrounded by containers. My final thought was of the work that still had to be done to move. It seemed insurmountable. I was placed, ever so carefully, on my bed with an ice pack held to my head and cried myself to sleep. Every corpuscle of my being ached with sorrow and shame.

Tuesday, August 19

Once again, my family has decided that I am in denial and need to seek out a support group that will provide me with the tools I need to stop fighting this disease and accept my horrible condition. I listen quietly and respectfully to them because they speak from a point of concern. They care, but for me, they are so off the mark and their concern becomes almost detrimental for me. I know in my heart of hearts that every action is thought through prior to the action resulting in my stealth behavior. Being cautious does not always result in a surreptitious movement. I wonder if they were attempting to conduct an intervention and again, with respect to their efforts, I say thank you. Even my immediate family/friend circle does not quite understand my daily pain and nighttime suffering.

Maybe it is my present 'peachy' reply that they have come to understand is a hypothetical answer to an abstract question. Whenever I am asked a general and concerned question regarding my health, I usually simply reply with a short and sweet answers, "I am peachy." That light and airy, sometimes humor response does not lend itself to conclude or equate to my nonacceptance but rather, for me anyway, admittance that I have not yet thrown in the towel. Not now, anyway but knowing is agony.

Saturday, August 23

We are neighbors/friends with another couple who also live in the woods. It is Saturday morning and we properly refer to it as "Dump Day". We join them when he discards the empty boxes once he removes its contents. After bringing his cut-up boxes to the dump, we go to breakfast and catch up on the happenings of the week. My husband has been working with him for a while now, just helping bring boxes or check on some old mail. He doesn't ask a lot, but it helps keep my husband active while giving him a function and purpose. They needed each other and each helped the other in their own way.

It is almost time to move and I am saddened. Our friendship thrived and we were only two doors apart. We shared some fun times, impromptu moments, and some quickie dinners outside on nice days. Remember, we lived in a glorious setting, and are close enough to throw a dinner together without pretense. I am certain our friendship will continue, but I am also certain that living so close together will be and already is missed by all four of us. I especially loved to joke with the husband and even still today refer to him as "the Olde Coote." We laugh, and he knows I love saying that phrase. Friendships, so late in life to such a close degree, are priceless and should be cherished. We all feel the same.

Sunday, August 24

Everything is in order for us to close on the sale of our glorious home backing to the woods followed by the closing on our one-level country club home. My husband and I have been traveling to our new home each morning around 3:00 AM. Each haul, we bring breakables and certain items that are too fragile to go on the moving truck. We stop at a diner after our drop and omit any rush-hour traffic.

Everyone around me, can see an improvement and I am suddenly maneuvering without hesitation. My appearance, they tell me, has some color and I no longer have dark circles under my eyes. With any luck at all, the Betaseron is kicking in and for the first time, I feel like myself.

For a long time now, it did not matter to me how I dressed or how I looked. I wore no makeup at all. Today, I can think clearly and do not feel like I am constantly in a fog. Whatever the reason, I feel human; that sums it up the best—feeling human and feeling alive.

This is the week I would be required to be back at school preparing my classroom for the soon-to-be-arriving students. Preparing the classroom, the physical room, would involve removing all of the protective newspaper or plastic garbage bags that I put up in June. The computers had to be covered, the flag was down, rolled up for its protection, and everything else in the room, bookcases, etc., had to be covered up for the summer. I can not imagine setting up my classroom at this level of my MS. The process can easily be described as indomitable and overwhelming.

Before the start of school, the classroom had to be set up again, uncovering, reconnecting and organizing before the children arrive the day after Labor Day. Every year, whatever my job or capacity was, I utterly despised the month of September. My lackluster attitude astonished all who knew me, knew of my dedication and my sincerity. Only a teacher can understand the difficult month-long "Start of School."

The start-up month of September and close-out month of June are both physically and mentally draining. There have been many who have joked with me, predicting my September as Doomsday. Their foresight paralleled the sad epic of a teacher without a classroom. I did not miss dark mornings, creating bulletin boards, setting up class registers, or the constant trail of students who arrived in school well into the month of September. I asked if they just moved to town, silently wondering where they were for the early part of September, the opening of school.

The children that didn't just move to town were the students who were on an extended vacation and just returned yesterday. I often wondered what these types of families thought about our education system and why it might be failing us? The teachers were here well before school opened, preparing for the opening of school.

Friday, August 28

It has all finally happened! We have moved into our new home. So much has happened this week with regard to moving because the closing dates had to occur on the same day, but my buyer was out of the country. He wouldn't allow his attorney to close it with a power of attorney and I started getting terrible vibes that this closing was being delayed purposely. Before my nerves could get the best of me, dates were selected, agreed upon, money exchanged hands, keys were exchanged, and it was over.

Now, I look around at my new home, rolling green hills, and applaud at its beauty. It is quite different than "My Woods" from the townhouse, especially with the changing seasons, but it is beautiful nonetheless. The best part is one level. No more steps.

I am feeling better and it seems amazing to me. Despite delayed and chaotic closings, here I am in my new home. I am amazed at how much clearer I can think, and for these last few days, I have not fallen. I have almost forgotten what it feels like to walk upright, straight, and without hesitation with every step I take. Now, I look down when I walk, frightened and almost hunched over.

I was able to go with my husband to purchase a LCD television and to another store to buy a stand for the TV. My stepdaughter's bridal shower is soon, and I was able to go to a third store to purchase the very last item I needed for the favors for her quests.

Thursday, September 4

Everyone that I have encountered in these past few days has noticed and commented on how well I was moving and walking. It feels awesome to be able to function without the overwhelming sense of fatigue. I accomplish more in a shorter period of time and it feels great.

Perhaps the intravenous treatment has kicked in, perhaps that the move is over, perhaps the drudgery of not getting up at 5:30 AM, perhaps this or that; I can only say "Thank You" for allowing me these couple of days of functioning as I once could.

Saturday, September 6

Almost all of the boxes are unpacked, and there is some sense of order in our new home. All of my seven working files are now completed and closed. Most of the new furniture has arrived and has been put in its place. It is a beautiful day and we are sitting on our patio drenched in sunshine, fresh air, and a feeling of satisfaction. It is quite beautiful here.

Tuesday, September 9

I have experienced the feeling of normalcy for most of the hours of the last few days. Unfortunately, today is not one of those days and this is not one of those hours. Both of my legs have that sense of heaviness, and I am unable to move my feet at all. It is , as always, a frightening experience. My brain is telling my legs to move, my toes to wiggle, or my feet to dance; it is just not happening. My silent fears can't be silenced. I sob quietly alone.

Friday, September 11

What was, what is now, and what could be have played repeatedly in my mind. I can't stop that voice asking the same questions over and over again. I had a taste of how I was before, and it felt wonderful.

I have had moments of how my future will play out and am always concerned about my level of functionality for the day. When I get one of those tremendous frontal headaches, I become scared of losing my vision. If my husband asks if my day was better, I always lie and tell him it was a good one. That is, I attempt to brush his questions off, but he knows me well enough to know how my day will go solely by looking at me. I am long past the days of "I am peachy." He is my husband and understands and listens to my every syllable, he is long past my words and appearance. We are two people that have morphed into one.

Sadly, deep in the crevices of my brain along with the constant pull on the broken strings in my heart, we know. Our good times need to be celebrated so the bad times can be tolerable. That is the one thought that keeps us moving in the direction of forward. Multiple Sclerosis is a disease that honestly, can be described as being different in every sufferer. When someone reassures me that tomorrow I will feel better than today, tells me that they really do not know anything about this auto-immune disease. I want to shout out, "Today is better than tomorrrow!" There can only be more legions on my brain, never less. Even I understand but refuse to focus on the negative.

Sunday, September 13

My Godparents came today to see our new home. I was so happy to see them. Last year they had given me a little red "Scooter-About" cart that I drive around. I usually take Misty out for some exercise and fresh air; she runs alongside of me while I drive my toy in my new neighborhood. The scooter allows me the freedom to move around, since my ability to ambulate is limited to just a few steps.

It has become difficult to balance myself without falling; sometimes I just drop to the floor for no apparent reason. Those falls are the ones where I land directly on my kneecaps. I have no warning and no notice. One second I am standing, and the next sound you hear is me hitting the floor hard with knees first.

Everyone is warning me to stop standing or walking. Their directive sounds somewhat abrupt: "*Be* careful! What will you do, God forbid, if you break your hip or a kneecap?" What exactly does *BE careful* mean? Never stand, never try to take even one small step and fear the worse, "God forbid," that I could break a bone or two? How do those spoken words help me? I am certain their intent is a positive one, but how *do I NOT* be careful? Am I attempting to dance? Perhaps they are afraid that I will attempt to jump rope. What are they thinking?

The answer is a simple one, one that I have grappled with for months. Disabled persons warned me of people's prejudice against those that are handicapped in one way or another. Discriminated against? Why? When I quickly tell them that I have never experienced such behaviors, they are quick to reply, "Just wait, you will see, it will happen, you have been lucky so far." "Trust us," they insist, "you will see!"

I had only hoped that I never feel the hurt and anguish that those others have felt. My marriage is healthy despite our hourly, daily, or weekly upheavals. My family and friends have been more supportive than I could have ever imagined. I was sad when I had to leave my beautiful townhome and our friends and neighbors. My new home, friends and neighbors are also wonderful. I really am blessed.

People chuckle when they see me "walking" with my rainbow cane. They look past my gaited walk and smile as I go by. Fortunately, I have not felt disabled. People have been kind and considerate even as my disease progresses. I am still invited to lunch with friends, family holidays, and neighborhood functions. They continue to insist that I have been fortunate. Only time will tell. Do the disabled feel discrimination? Uninvited? Not welcome? I hope not. Only time will tell. Could it be that my life has been truly blessed?

SECTION II

TWO YEARS LATER

A considerable amount of time has passed, almost two years, since I first began to write this story, a simple story that comes out of the mind of a disabled person. Today, now after these years, my family and I can recognize that our future is going to be quite different than planned. My disease is bearing down of both of us and our future is blurred. Ours is an internal never-ending conversation that is never quieted. We need to plan every move we make and how we can get from point A to point B. After a time, it becomes a natural course of action to wonder about obstacles that we may encounter. Are there steps involved? Is the elevator close enough, and if standing is involved, do I need to bring my own transport chair? How about my walker with the instant seat? Will I suddenly need to sit, should we bring that too?

My mind is always afraid and always wondering. Will I awaken on the event day with the fatigued feeling, the feeling I parallel to "being run over by a truck and left on the side of the road"? What will I do if that feeling of numbness comes over me, the one where my legs are too heavy to move and every word I speak slurs into the next, rendering my speech comparable to a drunken person? I can hear myself slurring, and I know I need to find a way to end the conversation. What will my exit strategy be? Every venue is different, and I memorize the ladies' room and exits before I even sit down. How will I get out of the situation without being noticed? Question after question, worry after worry, every activity and every day, my inner voice is never silenced.

My Multiple Sclerosis has the undertones of dooming disaster. My entire right side appears smaller than my left. The frightening episodes of numbness last longer than before. Every occurrence is worse than the one before. I renew my driver's license to use simply as photo identification. My car has been sold, and I have not driven in a long,

long time. Initially, I missed my car and the freedom of independence that it provided. It was difficult for me when I was told not to drive by both of my neurologists. Today, even the notion of remembering where I am doing or trying to recall how to get home seems unimaginable. I undersand that selling it was my only option.

I still had my hot little red Prelude parked in my garage. Soon, I thought I would drive—not far, just to a local store. The conversation involved selling it since I did not drive. I put that conversation off for months, and my freedom rider Prelude remained in my garage.

Another few months came and went and I finally agreed, but the potential buyers had to go to my brother's home to inspect the car. My hot red Prelude was taken from my garage and driven to my brother's home.

That was my first step of dependence. My sister-in-law drove my hot red Prelude around town with the For Sale sign displayed in the window. Each time I went into our two-car garage with only one car without a second car, my affliction became more realistic and my heart became a little heavier. I spelled out the price I wanted for the car without any negotiations. The had a "take it or leave it" mentality; I could not handle haggling over price and refused to even discuss it. The car had low mileage and one owner.

As I look back, it truly was a life-altering struggle between reality and fiction. My dilemma involved my ability to be independent versus my dependency on others. The day my husband called and asked if his buyer could have the car checked out by his own mechanic, a normal course of action, I had to agree. The car was an extension of me. I had a difficult two hours to absorb the notion that my disease is spiraling downward.

The drama continued for a short time. He came home with money. My car was sold. My husband was prepared to discuss the transaction. I refused to discuss it any further, and I wondered if he understood my sadness on his own, without me telling him. People say they understand, but they really do not. It is not their fault. How could they understand? The entire scenario was just too painful. I have been swallowed up and have lost myself. I am my disease. Unfortunately, people don't see me anymore. They cannot get past my inability to ambulate or my inability to negotiate steps. I am so very frightened.

They say it was the worst winter in thirty years for the entire eastern seaboard. After the first thirteen-inch blizzard, with more snow on the way, my husband and I decided to take my brother up on his offer. He just bought a new home on the Southwest Florida coastline. The master bedroom and master bath are on the first-floor level. His home is lake side and each morning I woke up early enough to watch the sun rise over the water. I felt so very peaceful. We remained in Florida for over two months. It was the first time in a long time that I really had the opportunity to slow down and relax. I found beauty in nature. The gorgeous estate of Mr. Ford was the beginning. The awesomeness of the Banyan tree was the best medicine that any doctor could have prescribed. I was thrilled with the fig tree and it's above ground roots. I finally was able to breathe. I was surrounded by the beauty of nature.

My husband ordered an outside scooter and a motorized wheelchair for the inside of the home. I was able to ride around and function fairly well. We are going to begin to look for a condo in and around the Naples area. I am hoping to be able to buy something big enough for everyone to come and stay awhile and to get away from the cold ice and snow. I am guessing that a wheelchair would not do well on ice.

My mom has been diagnosed with Dementia. She lives in her own home with a caretaker six days a week, eight hours a day. My Godson also lives with her; he is on another level, but for everyone involved, his living with her provides us with some peace of mind. When and if the time comes that he moves out for any reason, my brother and I will have to rethink the entire situation. She, like me, cannot live alone anymore. It is an open-ended question that simply can't be answered on a hypothetical level; only time itself will provide the answer.

Now is the time for my husband and I to take some time for just him and I. Winter in Florida was our first step towards the years defined by all as the Golden Years. Let's ponder that thought, what the hell are the Golden Years?

I also wonder if those two months put us into another label of "Snowbirds" in combination the Golden Years lifestyle. Do these labels suggest that we are feeling more aches and pains? Do they include the constant disappearance of our car keys? How about that golden feeling of frustration when you have to stop and recall if you even still own the car? Holy Cow, I don't think I do. My favorite is trying to remember where I placed my cell phone. Do I even still have a cell phone? I dial my number and go in the direction of the ringing sound.

I am sure that you can easily add to the collection of misnomers that cause us to wonder if our "Golden" years may possibly be tarnished.

Life goes, and each and every one of us has problems—big ones, small, one, or good days, bad days. The key is how we conduct ourselves as afflicted persons and who we choose to surround ourselves with.

In closing, I wish for you to find peace with your illness. Seek out happy occasions or even small moments where you can hold your head up high and be proud of yourself for the endurance you have so very graciously handled and taken in stride. It is your internal conversations that need curtailing unless they are propelling you forward. Personally, as you have read by now, I am mad as hell, and that anger resurfaces each time I fall and need assistance to get up.

I have not personally experienced or witnessed any discrimination due to my disability. Fellow handicapped persons have assured me that discrimination against disabled persons does exist. I have only felt it in almost all of the public lavatories. Yes, one can feel the bias of discrimination from the moment you enter a public rest room. It has perhaps not happened to every one of us, for some reason or another. Discrimination is not a new concept. Apparently, I have not felt the pain of the bias they speak of, good for me.

Be well, Chuckle when you enter a public restroom. I hope you are lucky and find the one where the HC stall is the first one in the row of stalls.

Tory Sileo

SECTION III

Three Months Later

I was finished writing this journal. It felt completed to me and in the hands of the publisher. This final comment will complete my journey as I travel through life with a disability. I had been warned of the possibility of a prejudice against persons with obvious differences.

It has happened. I have been "uninvited" due to my Multiple Sclerosis. My awkward style of maneuvering creates a fear in observers that I am about to tumble over and fall. I see the stares, I feel their worries and I understand their concerns. Everyone around me is silently wishing that I would sit down so they can have freely have conversations without interruptions. I am a distraction because of my unsteadiness. In all honesty, I recognize the relevancy of their reservations.

I am only welcome in their homes with the following conditions. I must agree to be in my wheelchair most of the time. I must be escorted to their bathroom and escorted back to my chair. In this scenario, there is little chance of my falling and therefore, everyone's qualms about my presence would be put to rest. This, I also I understand.

Understanding does not negate the hurt I feel. I must abide by the rules of the host or stay out of their house. Their feelings were simply stated, albeit, very harshly and without an ounce of kindness. How can I enter this home and feel welcomed?

How do I not feel 'on display'? How can I feel comfortable when every movement I make results in a glaring stare? My caretaker has been deemed incompetent due to his lack of monitoring my every move. It is his problem he has been told, to be the one and only one, who is responsible for my ambulating. If he does not provide aid in a more responsible manner, he is also not welcomed to their home.

I cannot promise to sit in my wheelchair and only use their bathroom with an escort at my side and yet, I understand their apprehensions.

I just do not feel comfortable. It is comparable to the experience one would feel if they were living in a glass house.

Visiting their home again is something I just cannot under go. Their fears have sadly affected my heart and soul. I have had advance notification of their hesitant invitation. I have had the wind knocked out of me and never saw it coming. And, still I understand it. I feel pain and sorrow so deep that it has become difficult for me to begin to breathe again. And still, perhaps I understand it. I have the sensation of the pain a fighter might feel when he experienced an upper punch to his already broken jaw. I may comprehend their concerns but I simply and sadly know that I will not be able to suffer the atmosphere created as I walk or roll through their front door.

Three months ago, I felt very proud to claim my never having felt the pains of discrimination. Three months later, now today, it is obvious that the belief I had was naïve. I have undergone the worse sense of hurt. I have felt a pain that I have never felt before.

Yes, they were right, I would indeed feel the sense of being unwanted due to my disability. They told me. They warned me, they were right. My heart hurts. It has happened.

SECTION IV

THREE MONTHS
AND ONE DAY

I visited my mom yesterday in her home, along with my brother and two of his four children. As I have explained, she has dementia and we all wanted to spend some time with her. It is morning and I slept at her home, so she would wake up this morning, Mother's Day with some one with her, her daughter.

She has a small home, a modest cape cod style and my nephew resides in the upper level. He is my Godson and he was home for most of the night. I love him very much, we have a close relationship and we were able to spend a large part of the evening doing Aunt C's 'chitter and chattering'.

I woke up very early this morning and realized quite a few things. Every time I went to stand up for Misty, bathroom, water, whatever, she repeatedly spoke these words, "Sit down, I don't want you to fall'. Every time, every single time, she did not miss a single opportunity to utter that phrase.

The words she shouted are the exact same words I felt when I was informed of the conditions of my visit to the home that I expressed earlier. I woke up this morning, right now, as I type, with an understanding that there is little difference between those words easily shouted because she is my mother and feels that she has the right to say it in a warning tone and someone else laying out the parameters of my visit to their home. Individuals that are not my mom and feel they are not close enough shout out the warning and instead pass those uncomfortable facial expressions are very clear for me now. Be it verbal, spoken or non-verbal with a sort of facial expression signaling others in the room are expressing the same concerns and the exact same outcome.

This morning, it is clear to me, "Don't mind me, I am only this 6,000 gorilla sitting here in the corner of the room." This is just another hurtful example of my upcoming future. It is beginning to happen and will only worsen. I have MS, I am not MS, Yes, I may fall, how comfortable can I be now in these moments when the hostess is not strong enough to lift me or has children where my falling would frighten them?

I have MS and my world is getting smaller. I will keep fighting to live a normal life and enjoy the good when I can. I have more good than bad and that will be my motto for as long as I can. These moments are hurtful in the manner is which they are expressed. They are difficult and reach into my very being. I have always had the ability to put these types of items into their own box, sort of on a back burner.

I will be able to do that with this aspect. It just hit me too abruptly and rude without conversation. Every aspect of this disease has it's moments. This type of discrimination was one hell of a moment.

I leave you with one more discovery. Picture this if you can. I am in a public place and need to use the ladies' room. I had my scooter and usually can drive it right into the handicapped stall. There is a line of women also waiting for a booth. I ride down to the handicapped stall and discovered that it is in use. I patiently wait for the booth to become available for my use. I found the wait time to be extraordinarily long. I can see feet move under the stall; therefore my wait time continued. Finally, the stall door opened and a young 20+ woman exited the stall. Her idea of the use of the handicapped stall was one with it's own sink and mirror for her makeup and hair touch up. This was another one hell of a moment. On that final note, I will say 'Be Well and God Bless' for a final time.. I wish you health and happiness.

Tory Sileo

SECTION V

Find yourself a hobby—
Keep your Cognitive
Abilities Functioning

I Rediscovered My Interest
In Photography. Enjoy!

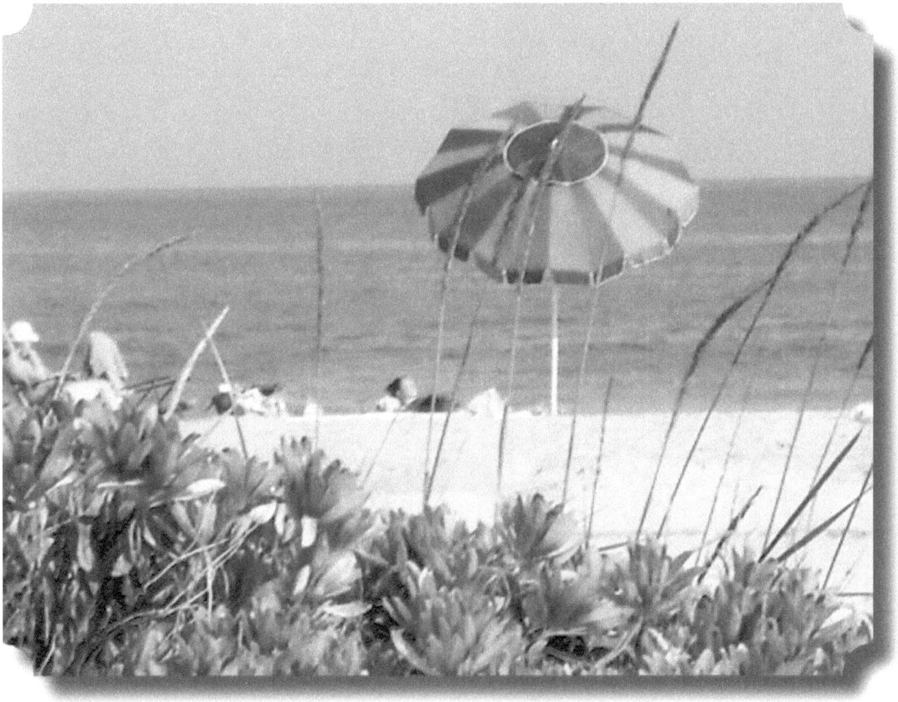

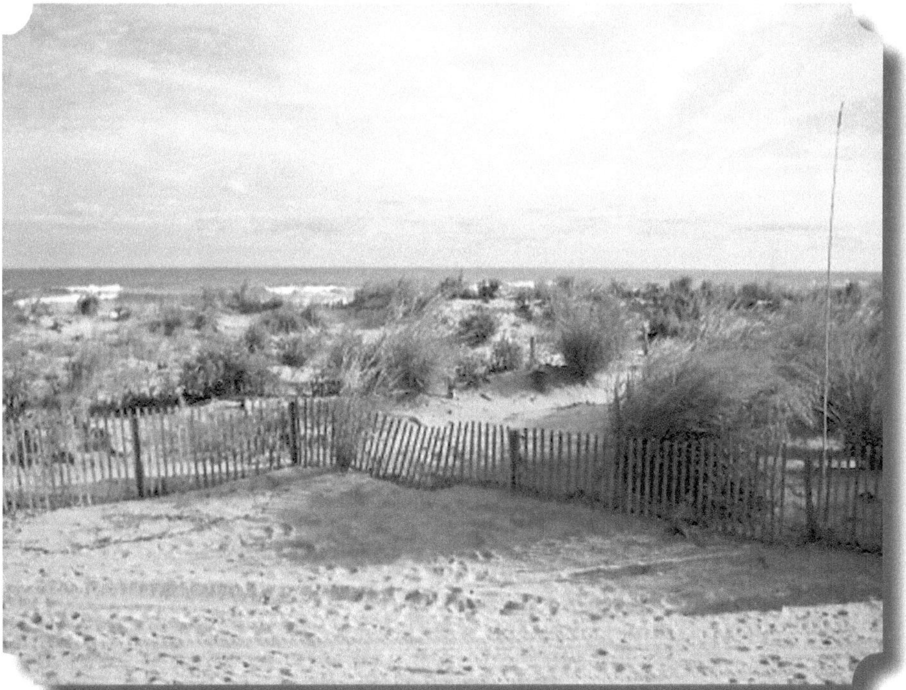

Index

www.ingramcontent.com/pod-product-compliance
Lightning Source LLC
Chambersburg PA
CBHW020342290526
45785CB00005B/2133